How to Master Your Practice

How to Master Your Practice

Dr. Charles Martin

MasterYourPractice.com

Contact Information

Charles W. Martin, Milestone Advisors
11310 Buckhead Terrace
Midlothian, VA 23113
(804) 241-0876
(804) 320-8708 (fax)
ISBN: 1981274243
ISBN 13: 9781981274246

Testimonials

Wow! The jewels in How to Master Your Practice not only reveal real truths of practice but also give you actionable ideas you can put to work. . It is one very power packed book. It is so good I will read it again. It's great for the advanced, experienced doctor to shed new light on problems and how to solve them. Moreover, for the younger doctor this really sets them on the right path.
If you want to continue to thrive, this book is a must-have for you and your team! "

Dr Straty Righellis
Oakland , CA

5 stars. An informative, quick read. It encourages and reinforces your entrepreneurial spirit. A must read for anyone wanting to get a leg up on the competition. It truly has assisted me increase the efficiency and productivity of my practice. Dr Martin shows you how to leverage the small and easily done into big dividends.

Dr L Douglas Knight
Orthodontist | Louisville, KY

"The title tells it all - How to Master Your Practice. Those who can roll with the punches of this economy, the evolution of patient expectations and diversity of marketing options required of a modern dental practice will find Charley's book fascinating. The first step in becoming is believing. His is a treasure trove of anecdotes and observations from inside and outside of dentistry that will set your mind on fire and possibly allow you to see yourself become a master dentist."

Dr. Bill Williams | Suwanee, GA

How to Master Your Practice is a must read for anyone attempting to survive and thrive in this ever changing environment of dentistry.
There are many consultants out there with information regarding practice management. Dr. Charles Martin's work has a distinctive advantage over those. The fact that he is a highly successful, practicing restorative dentist means he is living through the same challenges we are all facing.
He is a master teacher of dentistry and business. He understands the business challenges of dentistry and knows how to deal with them. His book is easy to read and understand. Most importantly, it will give you the tools you need to put your practice back on the path you want and deserve.

Dr Carl Roy
Va. Beach, Virginia

"My experience with Dr. Martin is that he has the knowledge and systems in place to help anyone's practice grow. He is one of the best in the industry."

Mark Elwell
San Diego, California

The fundamentals of running any business, any practice, are changing quickly. Our concentration upon procedures and commodities may jeopardize the future of our individual practices as corporations do the same on a grander scale. Dr. Martin's book How to Master Your Practice does not lament the changes. Instead, it harnesses those changes to create a new practice paradigm that is successful and has a right future. How do I know? Because Charley was my coach. If you are wondering what you can do to help your dental practice, or indeed, any business, read this book. It is a good read, entertaining and stimulating. This book can change your perspective and, more importantly, give you the answers to a stellar practice.

Dr. Lee Sheldon
Periodontist | Founder | The Institute for Dental Specialists

Charley is my coach, a mentor and a friend. His wisdom has helped me achieve what others only dream of, despite significant roadblocks. Charley has helped me clear the hurdles, steer around the potholes and dodge the bullets. This book and the nearly overwhelming amount of vital, relevant information it contains can help you too. You'll find this book to be a valuable guide and reference you'll want to continue to read over and over again. Keep it available as it will serve as a support system for your practice and your life. You need and deserve to have this information. Thank you Charley, Oh Wise One, for giving so much of yourself to me and our profession.

Michael J. Goldberg, DMD, FAGD, FIADFE, FACD, FNYAD
Manhattan Dental Health | New York City

"Overwhelmed tamed. Life regained." Quote from ***How To Master Your Practice***

This book is packed with feasible strategies and ideas for practice and business owners alike to help regain balance in their life. Insights are given into time management, marketing, growth, delegation, team building, client relationships, and productivity. Dr. Martin demonstrates how with clarity of purpose the right kind of hard work will bear fruit, and the importance of creating relationships with your clients and colleagues.

I read this book twice. I have post it notes tagged and will read it a 3rd time. I gained some great insight from it - and am already committed to increasing my "smart" work in 2018, and have already started delegating more to my team!!

This is a must read for anyone looking to hit the reset button in their business, and create harmony between work and home life!

Elizabeth Bogan
Denver. CO

Table of Contents

From the Desk of Dr. Charles Martin

Dear Reader and Fellow Dentist,

I am Dr. Charles Martin, but you can call me Charley. I have five adult children, five grandchildren and three grand-dogs, one of which, Cooper, steals my shoes and if not kept on a leash, runs away. I have been married to the same wife since 1977. Her name is Holly and she is extremely patient, quite understanding and the best teammate for life a guy could ask for.

While practicing, I have been coaching dentists and small business owners for over 30 years, teaching them my unique Master Your Practice System to practice growth, increased profits and professional success.

I have had an enviable practice emphasizing cosmetic makeovers and dental implant reconstruction. My practice statistics strike most dentists as unbelievable or unattainable. Yet, the combination of the mindset I bring to practice and my very sophisticated system for attracting the right patients and making successful case presentations to them is in fact teachable and replicable. I have done just that for many.

So I'm going to start out by describing my practice and life a little bit. Set aside skepticism and disbelief for now. Ignore "the reasons" and mental nay saying why you couldn't have this kind of practice for a moment. Squelch those "little voices" that cast doubt about me and your own ability to do what I do. Just consider whether you would like to have this kind of a practice if you could – a practice you have mastered.

First of all, you should know that I take at least ten weeks off every year, with my wife, and sometimes, with my whole family. The most recent trip was just shy of three weeks to Venice, Lake Cuomo, and Milan, Italy and then over to Athens and a yacht cruise in the Greek Isles. I have taken TWO YEARS off—21 months to be exact—to do some of the things I've always wanted to do, while my practice motored along without me because of the systems of operations I set up.

Now don't get me wrong, I do work. It's just that I don't suffer through the stress of not knowing what to do or how to do it. For me, the daily struggle is gone. I can get all the new patients I need, but I don't need a herd of 'em because of my high case presenta-tion success. I don't see a slew of patients every day. Often just one or two patients for the entire day.

I really enjoy my days of practice because I have trained my patients to appreciate what I do for them.

I have staff that are dedicated and committed to taking care of my patients and me, again because I have trained them why they should by building an authentic practice culture based on the heart – my practice purpose, soul – my practice values and goals of my practice. Shouldn't you do the same?

Personnel used to drive me crazy, but not anymore. I can show you how I have done it.

I built a practice that just about any dentist would lust for... and in the process accumulated several million dollars of real wealth, and a practice worth a couple million dollars more. To some of you – maybe you – a few measly million dollars isn't all that impressive. For many reading this, though, this is a very large number. It is such a big number that, bluntly, a number of you will never reach by following "The Norms of Practice" dictated by those who care not one iota about your personal success.

I also happen to know quite a few "Big Name Speakers" and so called "Heavy Hitters" of Dentistry who everyone thinks of as wealthy and successful, but who are, in truth, still in urgent need of next month production to meet last month's expenses, who will never see a million dollars all in one place in their lives – unless it's inside a glass display in one of those casinos in Las Vegas. Many of these now are the teachers and consultants to the profession!

Anyway, I might point out that I didn't come from money, I did not inherit a bunch of money nor did I have a rich uncle that gave me a huge trust fund. Relatively speaking, I was poor as dirt growing up. I can still remember having just one pair of pants to wear when I was a kid and those were hand-me-downs from my brother. That was long ago.

I am very good at what I do; but, certainly, few would consider me to be the best dentist that walks (frankly, I am not sure how that question would be settled). I am a Master of the Academy of General Dentistry, Diplomate of the Congress of Oral Implantologists and Fellow of the Academy of Dento-Facial Esthetics. I am also a Diplomate of the American Board of Implant Dentistry. I have spent close to 10,000 hours in training in clinical dentistry, leadership, management and marketing, thousands of those hours outside the field.

Why outside dentistry? Because that's where the answers were to the problems that vex and torment you as a dentist.

Had the answers been "inside that box of dentistry," you would have found them long ago.

I have gone "outside the box" of our proud profession so now you don't have to.

I am certified as a business growth coach in a unique system that sets atop your existing organization and turbochargers it for scaling up growth.

I am also certified as a coach in the next great business wave – the transition of businesses and practices to the next generation. This is the eventual reality all practices face and you should be prepared by knowing what to do to make your transition as valuable as it should be.

I really wasn't very good when I started out way back in 1979, but what young dentist is? I've learned, persisted and achieved my success by not listening to the limitations that others wanted to impose on me, but by training and evaluating the real truth about success in practice.

I have taught leadership, marketing, innovation, organizational design, scaling up business, practice growth, public speaking, sales, case presentation and communication. Over the past twenty years, I have consulted, coached and created programs for many different fields and professions: Lawyers, accountants, painting con-tractors, a pharmaceutical equipment manufacturer, mortgage brokers, mortgage bankers, a pest control company, internet tech-nology consultants, networking marketing experts, physical thera-pists, management consultants, marketing consultants, building contractors, and website developers.

I have helped them grow and manage their businesses to extract all the available profit and discover their hidden, underutilized hard assets and underdeveloped human capital. I have done the same for dental solo practitioners, orthodontists, group practices, Implantologists and other specialists in dentistry.

Let's Talk About You

I believe you should know what I think about dentists and orthodontists.

I believe dentistry is a noble profession. Mostly unrecognized by too many for all the good it does for the people we serve.

You should be particularly proud of what you do because of the lasting effects you provide for the lifetime of your patient.

While appearance is the obvious one, most patients do NOT know about the effects of dentistry and orthodontics on airways, growth, facial esthetics, joint health and resistance to both dental caries and periodontal disease for life.

Yours is a transformational health service that has too little acknowledgement, appreciation and understanding. You make life-changing effects and create better, longer lives for your patients. This is why I am so proud to work with dentists and orthodontists as a business coach and practice profits advisor.

I believe you want to make a difference. You want to help people. You want to help make better lives for those people called patients and all those around you. Your work matters. This is recognized by cultures worldwide with your title, Doctor.

Many others in business do not have such a clear and constant purpose. They strive for success and then figure out how to be significant.

Right from the beginning, your work makes you significant to society. But you have a huge problem; the success that should be yours is increasingly more difficult. And it will get worse. Much worse. Why?

Running your practice beyond the delivery of care has been an afterthought for too many doctors in the dental profession for too long. It has been a conglomeration of ideas and concepts that never really fit together. When money was plentiful, ineffective and inefficient methods of running your practice didn't seem to matter much. Not anymore.

What was once enough in running your practice has morphed into the increasingly unworkable. The new reality is the old way of practice is broken. How did that happen?
Society and technology have changed. Our culture has changed. People have changed. Change is the constant that most practitioners shun. Some embrace the technology changes, but virtually none embrace the whole of the changes.

Big money and Wall Street have entered our field. More are coming – fast. Wall Street has discovered the profits that practices have, if operated differently. And like other fields in healthcare, cottage industry thinking that pervades dentistry surrenders ultimately to the bigger and better organized.

Frankly, the dental profession as a whole missed seeing this future. They missed the trend.

You, like most practitioners, did not see it coming. Few have responded to it, as they should. Now your choices are to ignore it (dangerous!) or get smart and operate your practice by design-instead of haphazardly. Just know this: you can't do it the way it has been done in the past.

Practitioners in dentistry have always been seekers of some new opportunity, some new shiny "thingy" to make money without really recognizing the futility of this way of thinking and being. They think of operating their practices as a patchwork of bits and pieces – not a strategic system of operating. It is a trap. These bits and pieces don't really fit each other and never do the real job. I call this OSD – Opportunity Seeking Dentist – always looking for the magic bullet, yet even when found, that bullet disappoints.

Still hope springs eternal, "Maybe the next one," the opportunity-seeking dentist says. This is what drives much of the purchase of the latest in technology and course taking.

The preference for many dentists is to fix whatever problem symptom comes up by taking another clinical course. This is just another way to avoid really handling what the real problem is. I understand. Once upon a time long ago, I did that myself.

The Master Dentist on the other hand, looks to have a coherent whole – creating a practice by strategic design, not some mish-mash of bits and pieces that never get the job done and makes you feel overwhelmed and unhappy.

The Master Dentist knows that these bits and pieces and the latest silver bullet only serve to make him feel constantly behind. The Master Dentist has clarity and focus that lets him let go of the unimportant, freeing him from mind clutter.

The Master Dentist concentrates on the things that matter and leaves the rest. He leverages his time and actions and happily delegates the rest by design. He has the knowing confidence of knowing what to do and none of the angst and anguish of that too many OSD doctors endure.

The Opportunity Seeking Dentist works harder and harder to make things work. But hard work alone is not the answer. You know that by experience. Yet, somehow you may feel that you aren't doing it right. That it is your fault that your practice isn't working like you want. No, it is not. Your intentions are pure, your lack of design and strategic approach doom you from the beginning despite your good intentions.

You see the signs daily. You feel the overwhelm. You hear yourself saying that it's your own fault. It's exhausting.

What the opportunity-seeking dentist does with his practice as a business, he would never do with his patient and that patient's treatment plan. When you are treating patients you design a strategic plan that takes all factors into account and execute that plan to get results predictably. You wouldn't dare treat without diagnosis and a solid treatment plan. To do otherwise is a big no-no. It is malpractice.

For the opportunity-seeking dentist, they treat their practice as a mish-mash of pieces and parts without a real plan, without a coherent system that predictably gets results. This is but another form of malpractice – organizational malpractice! It doesn't work and you know it doesn't. How can I say that? Are you making all the money you want? Are you feeling good about where you are in practice right now? Are you getting all the new patients you want? For virtually every dentist, the answer is no.

For many their solution is "I'll just work harder," – what if you are working as hard as you can already? How long can you keep that up?

The common lament is "I haven't got time." Everyone has the same amount of time. If you haven't got time, you are spending your time working on the wrong thing.

For the opportunity-seeking dentist (OSD), disappointment is almost a natural state. This takes its toll. It feels like your psyche is getting attacked from all sides. You have near constant money pressure from not getting the results you want while spending more time and more money to try to achieve them using this bits and pieces concept that you can already see does not work.

At the same time, your work is difficult. Straining. Isolating. You question yourself and what you have done. You wonder if the sacrifices you have made in time and money would have been better spent on yourself and your family doing something you would have enjoyed instead of the depressing mess called your practice.

Be careful here. Don't be too hard on yourself. No one ever handed you the directions to operate your practice. Your directions were missing.

The Master Dentist knows that he has to create TWO results: the delivery of fine care to his patients and the creation and nurturing of the organization that provides it (that's the part that gets missed).

Few dentists really recognize the importance of the second phrase: creating the organization that delivers it. The Master Dentist gets it. He understands and so he has a very different experience with his practice.

When doctors do not design their practices with strategic thinking, they just jump in and by default they end up building their practices around themselves. But building a practice or a business around the owner leads to the owner owning a job. And the reality becomes that the doctor doesn't own the practice, the practice owns him.

Opportunity seeking dentists fail and fumble on their current and future income. They get wornout. Some just quit. Many have no real plan for retirement. Many simply can't afford to transition because they need the income and their practices just aren't worth enough to retire on.

For the Master Dentist, reality is quite different. Success is his calling card. His future is virtually assured. His experience is that procrastination fades, resistance fades and dare I say it, a level of happiness pervades.

Imagine waking up and you can't wait to start your day.

Imagine feeling that sense of professional accomplishment at a spiritual level.

Imagine having a practice that affords you the freedom to choose your lifestyle on your terms because you have all the money you need. Can you see it?

Overwhelm tamed. Life regained.

Wasn't this the dream you had when you went into practice?

This book is designed to help you outthink, outcompete, and outwit the competitive forces in your environment so you can win. The fact that you are reading proves that you are working to win, too.

This book is meant as a guide to give tools and perhaps alter the course of your practice and entrepreneurial life for the better. I hope that this book will help lead you to better mastery. May the words here help you combine new innovative thinking to your natural "smarts." I salute your continuing dedication to becoming a master of your business, your practice, your craft. I use the term craft here to mean the application of your knowledge, understanding, and wisdom to your work.

Unfortunately, you, like everyone else, have blind spots. These are the things that you don't see, because you are too close to them or just aren't aware.

You have more challenges. It can be darn lonely being a dentist. You need to work with people of like mind, associate with those who understand how you think. This can be a challenge! (And I have a solution at the end of this book, for those who seek more.)

Thank you in advance for the honor of being your guide through my own life experiences and training, which I share with you in this book. I've learned this through the crucible of everyday living and my own extensive study, in my many years of professional practice as a dentist, and as a business growth coach. An unusual combination admittedly, but one I've enjoyed a great deal.

I've written this book in digestible bites because these pages are meant for busy people like you who often don't have time for reading for long periods of time. This book has been designed to make it far easier for you to consume.

Have fun. Enjoy the adventure of this book. May you become a Master Dentist. All the Best,
Dr. Charles Martin

We help Dentists and Orthodontists create a different kind of practice with a steady, consistent, predictable flow of new patients who want to say yes to your best care so you make more money without the frustration and overwhelm.

MasterYourPractice.com

Preface

You have before you a handbook to be used as an owner's manual for the entrepreneur and professional. Created from the rough material of personal and business experience, this book is intended to give you close, real, street-level perspective and guidance. So sometimes it's very personal. Sometimes it isn't pretty. Sometimes it's painfully honest, stern, playful, and hopeful. I would hope that it rings true to you. And I'd hope it will help bring you closer to the places you dream of going in your life and practice.

When reading this book it should be kept in mind that it is compiled from the weekly memos that I produce for my practicing clients. These writings were firmly intended to be read, understood, and most importantly, implemented. In my client groups, change for the better isn't an option or a goal, it's the expected outcome of inspiration and action.

The Stupid Tax

When he spoke, the room grew quiet. What he said next gave the entire assemblage one of the biggest ah-has of the entire conference.

First, he related how he had tried to go it alone and how much he had spent. It was nearly fifty thousand a month promoting his business. His tone foreshadowed his next words.

"I had been paying the stupid tax month in and month out because I thought I could go it alone. Yet when I finally did get the advice and consulting I needed, my promotion spend dropped to twenty-five thousand a month with better results."

John's admission created more than a little buzz in the room as each member of the crowd reflected on his own life and the stupid tax he had paid on more than one occasion.

For the throng, it was one of those unexpected learning moments—a treasure that made the entire day worthwhile all by itself.

How many forms of the stupid tax have you seen others pay? Have you paid yourself?

First, the definition of stupid tax: the money, time, energy, or effort you paid or lost needlessly. The stupid tax is an error that costs you but shouldn't. Clients pay this toll repeatedly—waiting until the problems are so bad that the time, energy, and expense to repair them mount to thou- sands or tens of thousands of dollars. Over time, this can amount to millions of dollars.

The tax is paid when one keeps doing the same thing over and over, expecting a different result. The tax is levied against one when one fails to act when one knows one should. The tax is extracted from one's bank account when one tries to go it alone when one is not an expert in a field when one needs an expert.

This "unnecessary fee" is paid when one fails to implement what works. The tax comes due when one tries to go cheap when one shouldn't.

The tax gets paid when patience is required and impatience reigns. The tax is paid when one doesn't nurture one's patient leads and doesn't continue to communicate with both leads and existing patients.

The stupid tax is life's way of teaching us lessons—hopefully only once instead of several times over.

Do you know someone who is paying one now? Can you help them?

How You Lead

Leadership

A New Look

To lead or not to lead, is not the question.

If you are in charge of anyone else, your JOB is to lead. Take a moment and let that concept settle. Roll it around with your mind tongue. Let your intellectual taste buds check it out. Ask your emotional teeth to sink into that.

If you are in charge of anyone else, it is your duty to lead. Leadership is part of life. It is vital to your success and those that count on you to lead.

Strangely, many people who should lead choose to ignore the responsibility to lead, usually by omission—not doing what should be done.

Key point: your team members need direction. Real leaders give it. The best ones give a lot more.

Followers deserve a leader. Factually, it is treason to fail to lead when you are "it." Too many people depend on you and your direction to pretend or shun the work of leading. Followers leave those who do not lead or lead badly. Groups can thrive with good leaders. They will surely wither with poor ones.

Many see leadership as a burden. Others revel in it. How you frame the virtues of leadership in your mind determines much of your willingness and success with leading. Too many believe the negative voices within that make you question your ability to lead. Ignore those, please. Everyone has them. Once you really decide on your direction and then commit to it, those nagging, self-defeating voices die away. They become powerless. But if you doubt, those voices can reach a deafening crescendo that drowns out any hope of giving direction to yourself and others and leaves you meandering around wondering what is happening to you. Moreover, the members of your group look for someone to follow. An unled group is ripe for loss of the fabric of the group—its members.

So what are the duties of your duty to lead?

Groups need leaders to set the values, purposes, goals, strategy, and standards of the group, including the ethical example. Your group needs the same.

Values are simply the guiding beliefs and principles you live by as a practice or a business. Taking the time to write them is time well spent. Personally, I have defined seven core values with a number of secondary principles.

* Make a Difference
* Do Whatever It Takes
* Guidance
* Performance
* Spirit of Play

* Own the Ownership Mentality
* Make Momma Proud

Naturally, these take a bit more explanation, but these are the guidons, the small guiding flags that identify us.

Purposes are simply why you do what you do. What is the higher reason for you to be in practice or in business? Akin to your beliefs, these purposes are about how you make a difference for those you serve.

Goals are the direction for you and your team to take to live the values and purposes. Neglect these at your peril. Without these you can get a lot of activity without accomplishment. While goals are part of the sacred trust of successful living, don't hold them in so much reverence that you fail to make them for fear of setting the wrong ones. Heck, these can change and should change as you live and practice. Set them and don't forget them.

Strategy is the overall plan designed to help you accomplish your goals. Strategy done well is living, breathing, ADAPTING to the environment and marketplace. Life is much the same. One must change to take the advantage given in a situation. The greatest leaders of history were marked by their amazing ability to seize these titular moments when they came.

Strategy is about what you are going to do and how you are going to do it spoken in broad strokes. The details come later in specific plans of execution.

Standards are the guiding rules of "how we work around here." These include the rules and policies, along with expectations of performance, both as an individual member of the group and as a team member. Too often these go wanting. These rules of action are requirements for a cohesive team who agrees to them. Without agreement, you do not have a team. The synergy is lost.

That synergy is the secret sauce of groups to accomplish more together than is possible as unaligned individuals.

Agreement with these standards is part of the process of becoming and staying a member of the group. Those who cannot agree cannot be part of the group. Simple. Sometimes these policies do change, but only for a good reason.

Leading a group that is aligned with the defined values, purposes and goals of a group is a great joy. A poorly led group is a vessel of sorrow.

There is good news. You get to decide. What will it be?

Can You or Anyone "Manage" a Team?

We were driving to our weekend cottage on Rappahannock River when my wife read an article aloud from our newspaper. It was about keeping and managing the "twenty-something" age workers. The following is a reasonable facsimile of that conversation.

"Listen to this, Charley," spoken not quite commandingly, but with enough emphasis that I knew I should listen up if only to be a "good listener husband."

"This group is not loyal to the employer or corporation, but to themselves. They saw what happened to their parents who were loyal only to be jettisoned during re-engineering management spasms. They want to be engaged, to be creative. Money is not as important to them as possibly a gift certificate or time off even without pay."

"What do you think of that?" my wife asked.

"The article is correct and there's a lot more to it," I replied.

She detected a long dissertation coming. She left the article and continued her reading. It got me thinking.

My experience with team members of all ages is that they all want to be engaged—to be part of something that has meaning, to make a contribution. They want to be creative and to work together.

* The more noble and high flung the purposes and goals of the group, the more commitment and energy they bring to the job.

This principle of working with people is vital to your success. The better you are able to tell the story of what you do and why you do it, the easier it is to manage any group. The ones that agree with you and your compelling future are easier to work with, more fun, and more productive. Those who do not agree will find ways to get in the way and, sometimes, torment you. Sometimes they do this overtly, but more usually, covertly. Detecting the disagreement can be more than a small challenge, because they often hide their true intentions.

* Productive working relationships are built, expanded, and empowered based on agreements.

Your job is to create your unique story and continue to tell it repeatedly, with all the original passion from which the story sprang. As a leader for your group, this is job one. Team members who don't buy-in will either find another position on their own or reveal themselves with their deeds and words. You should remove those who don't buy-in no matter how valuable they may seem. Those who disagree create more disagreement from their interaction with other team members.

Jack Welch, in his book Winning, described his view of person-nel. To him there is the top 20 percent, the middle 70 percent, and the bottom 10 percent. The top 20 percent are the achievers who should be rewarded exceptionally. The middle 70 percent are the most management demanding and the bottom 10 percent should be removed. This dropping of the bottom 10 percent, in his view, was the most merciful of actions, for it helped the under-achievers find other positions with other companies where they could be achievers. Additionally, it freed the company from wast-ing dollars and time with those who did not contribute.

This is another version of the 80/20 rule—again. Team members that are not performing to your standards are like a heavy weight that holds a hot air balloon down. Remove the weight and watch the balloon (your practice) soar. There is a very important point to make before you decide to remove someone: ensure you have done everything you could do to help the team member to buy-in and to be successful.

I leave you with these three questions:

* Do you have a bottom 10 percenter that you have not been able to coach to improved performance and living and inspiring others with your practice values?
* Knowing what you know now, who on your team would you not re-hire?
* Now, what should you do?

Can You Keep Good Team Members Engaged?

How do you treat and handle your top 20 percent of your team? If you assume that they will continue to do well without paying attention to them, you are making a serious mistake. Ask me why I know. Only a small percentage of the general population does not need acknowledgement or rewards. Just because you don't need many strokes, doesn't mean that others don't.

If you are like most, you will treat your best performers like every other team member, ignoring the very people that make it possible for you to enjoy the success you have.

Does your experience teach you that a few key people are responsible for the majority of your success? Mine does. I don't necessarily like it that way, but that seems to be the way life works— and not just in dentistry, but every field. You see this easily in sports. LeBron James made the Miami Heat and then Cleveland Cavaliers winners almost overnight. Every field has stars. The difference between the star and the regular team member is in the results that they produce.

Stars know they are good. They love to be measured. They are proactive. They like to be involved. They want to be creative. They think about your practice and how it can be better. They enjoy what they do. They love to be led by a worthy leader.

Should you treat your stars differently? I say yes. Base your rewards on performance that is measurable and objective. Give them your attention and interest. Usually the opposite occurs. Your poor performers drain all your energy out and your best people go without.

You manage your best people differently than your average people. It is more of a coaching role than a management role. Talented people are often easier to handle because the work you do with them gets results; it's not wasted time and effort. Your coaching is rewarded by seeing your people grow, along with the results they produce.

How should you reward your stars? Ask them. It may take several requests orally and in writing to get what these are. Have them make a list of rewards they like and work out how they can get them based on exceptional performance that is measurable. High performers love to play the game of performance. Set big targets with your stars.

Remarkably, if you measure carefully, you'll find the cost of having your stars is less than your average team member. Yes, their pay will typically be higher, but so are the results they produce!

They enjoy mentoring relationships. Conceptually, a mentor is much like the Jedi Master from Star Wars movies—who pokes, prods, teaches, guides, questions and, most importantly, cares about the person. You should not be the only mentor if you have stars. In fact, one of the privileges of being a star is being a mentor.

Your stars take responsibility for making results happen. They take the initiative. They dislike non-performers although they may not tell you outright. They get more results when non-performers are removed from the group. In my experience, your top performers are looking for you to make the tough decisions that are expected of leaders. When you do make them, their respect for you grows. When you don't, the opposite is true.

Procrastination on your part is seen as a sign of weakness.

Invest some time and effort in finding out about them, what they like, what spurs them on. Give them training in the areas for which they have talent. Ensure they get to work at positions that match their strengths. Ask them for help in finding other high performers. Give bonuses and rewards. Pay attention to them. Praise them in the style they like (be it public or private). Listen to what they have to say. Find creative ways to say thank you. Be their friend.

Do be careful with giving time off. Time off works against your interests when used as the main reward for performance. I am speaking in terms of weeks, not a day here or there.

Your regular performers will see and hear about the perks of performance and work to become a star. Your treatment of your stars sets a good example for the behaviors and results for your middle two-thirds (average performers).

Is age a factor? Maybe—but it is not the factor most people think. Stability is an issue. Often the "twenty-somethings" are very unsettled.

Personnel going through turbulent personal times (divorce, death of a parent or child, other per- sonal losses, etc.) are often unstable for months or years.

Talent is the factor that is critical. Certain personality types are better suited for various positions. An easy comparison is the personality of a bookkeeper versus a dental assistant. These are two distinctly different types. A very good bookkeeper would be miserable as a chairside assistant.

Trainability is important. Willingness to learn is important. Willingness to be coached is an issue. What they can contribute is important to them also. They look first to challenge and contribution rather than what is in it for them. Your best people do expect higher pay and perks but are willing to prove their worth. They are passionate about what they do. "I love my job" is a common refrain they utter.

Systems and Teams

Should you base your personnel on a star or a system? The answer is both. The problem with stars is that aren't enough of them and sometimes they are just too darn expensive. So, you can't get dependent on your stars to make your practice or business work.

* The ideal is a system of actions that ordinary people can use to get extraordinary results.
* Adding a star to a good system can increase results significantly.
* Make stars by training and coaching.

Keep your best people doing what they do best.

The only objectors to performance-based rewards are from those who do not perform at a high level. A favorite statement is that "everyone is equal." Bull!

Your non-performers will complain, gripe, and/or quit. Know them by their actions first. If there is a hint of disharmony going on within your team, look first to your non-performers—they are most likely to spread gossip and breed discontent. Further, non-performers try to hide their results or not be held accountable for what they are supposed to do. When confronted, they are the most adroit at providing excuses.

How do you know that your removal of a person from your team was a good one? Four ways:

* Your current team says, "What took you so long?"
* The former team member's name disappears completely from conversations.
* Productivity increases.
* The effort it takes to make things happen is far less when you remove a bad egg. Your daily work flow goes easier, and is less stressful.

Stories, Connection and Influence

"Right, you are!" I exclaimed as I semi-ran to the front of the room while leading the applause. It was another evening of teaching a public speaking and human relations course. This student had just finished his two-minute talk meant to teach a lesson using a story. He had told a personal story of his grandmother and cooking biscuits in her farmhouse when he was a little boy.

The formula was simple: tell a story for 1 minute 50 seconds and use the last 10 seconds to make your point and give the benefit. Yes, the story absolutely dominated the time. And it should have. The story instantly got attention. Stories do that.

Stories are among the building blocks of our culture. We tell stories to our children. As a parent, who hasn't heard that little diminutive voice saying, "Read me a book," at bedtime, with the simultaneous tug on your leg. Stories are woven into the fabric of our society and have been for a very long time. In many ways, stories are our preferred way to receive our communications. What would you rather receive: a well-told story or a list of facts displayed on a PowerPoint presentation?!

Sure, the student could have merely made his point and given a benefit of following the point or lesson. Blah. That never works. It is insulting to the listener. It sounds like a platitude that virtually no one can abide. The words delivered as such violate the basic contract of human communication: give value to the listener. Facts without a story stand naked in the cold, unwelcomed into our souls.

The value of a story is given both in message content and the quality of the delivery. The storyteller who skimps on one or both of these devalues his listeners. The reality is that the audience, whether one or one million, wants the storyteller to do well. A well-told story wends its way through the ears and into the audience's minds virtually unfiltered. What other form of communication can do that?

Stories are the agreed-upon voice that is welcomed in cultures around the world. Great story- tellers are admired and given more than a little reverence. They can become novelists, screenwriters, speechmakers, military brass, successful entrepreneurs, professionals, and corporate leaders. Ministers and political leaders are lost without an ability to tell stories that capture the hearts and minds of their listeners.

Stories are a sort of preferred proof that humans place on the scales of decision because they bring us a chance to relate, agree, and then support the point made. Good stories give an almost unfair advantage because they are "the wanted way" to receive a message.

What else about stories makes them the deliverer of votes and dollars and romance? Stories add dimension and personality to figures, facts, and stats. They make these bloodless, lifeless numbers real to the emotion centers and thus enable the logical mind and its decision centers to become functional. Remove those emotion centers from the cognitive mind and you'll render the person unable to decide even the most mundane of the daily decisions. Fail to speak to these emotional physiologic centers located in the frontal cerebral cortex and you will not get a yes to what you suggest. (This is the reason that facts alone, logic alone, education alone, or science alone won't budge your patient.)

Make your life easier: tell a story. Just as testimonials and reviews of patients tell the stories of their successes with you or your product, the stories you tell elevate your status to those you presently serve.

Entertaining stories are given personal preference by your listener, for these bring life to his life. Bore no more and open the door to delighted people who want to be around you and send others to do the same.

What else do stories do for you? Let me relate a quick story. I am an avid reader. I read at least a book a week. On trips, I sometimes consume two or three or four.

I once thought that the way I could move ahead was to shortcut the process by reading book summaries. Nope. That didn't work for me. Why didn't it, you ask? Here's why: the stories are cut out. No good for me. The stories leave an emotional imprint that has the point or benefit message attached. With no story the facts fall into the abyss of words read but not remembered. Stories ensure your message gets across and recalled.

Why do you think all those bedtime stories and their lessons were created? To help shape young minds, of course. Well, the shaping hasn't stopped there. How many older minds are shaped by stories daily?

The point is that stories with lessons attached leave indelible marks in the minds of those who experience them by reading, listening, watching, or living them.

Stories have yet another unique ability. Storytellers who reveal themselves are able to deepen relationships with their audience unilaterally. The audience find themselves in the storyteller's saga and identify with the teller's challenges, woes, and victories. This creates a unique connection to the teller of the tale and builds a greater willingness to take the message to heart.

If you need to persuade others to your way of thinking, stories are the ideal way to bring your message to your public because stories pierce the marketing and sales defense system that virtually every human must erect for self-protection. Stories move unscathed into the hearts and minds of those you want to influence. Moreover, the story has the particular advantage of moving past the fortress walls of the emotional objection because the story, like the objection, uses emotion. This gives it that extra oomph so necessary to overcome what can be fierce resistance. When it comes to persuasion and influence, stories can render the "Walls of No" defenseless.

Back in my class, I, with deliberation, remarked about my student's story, the specific details shared and how he re-created the love for his family in the minds of his audience. I asked the class to give their "what he did right" points. They chimed in quickly with further affirmations of his performance. The speaker beamed with pride. His confidence giant-stepped three stairs that night.

That's the way that stories work and the way that humans work, too. What story do you need to tell?

Your Old Job Isn't Your New Job

The headline read, "Snagajob founder giving up day-to-day duties." Shawn Boyer, the founding CEO for 12 years at the time, stepped away from his position. It seems almost unfair. After all, he had propelled his start-up into success. He was a 2008 U.S. Small Business Administration's National Small Business Owner of the Year. Naturally, the newspaper article painted the change in role in the best possible PR terms. A founding CEO steps down to make way for an outsider to take over his duties so he can focus on strategy and long-term business development? Yes, and for good reason.

It happens all the time. A new start-up company rockets ahead and then sputters as it reaches new heights. Angel investors, who contributed cash to help get the business going, grow nervous. Venture capitalists who have provided two or more rounds of funding while gaining control of the company move in and replace the founding CEO with an experienced CEO that has traveled the path before on the road to IPO and the wealth that can accompany that.

What happened was that the founding CEO failed to recognize that he was constantly getting a new job. He held on as long as he was competent to hold the position, and characteristically, a bit longer.

Once he reached his limit, his span of control was no longer big enough for the company to thrive. Its new controlling interests, the venture capitalists, rode in, demoted the current CEO, and installed a new sheriff accustomed to a business with that size and complexity.

What does this have to do with you? Think about it for a moment.

It has everything to do with you if you run a professional practice or small business. Here's why: Your old job is not your new job once you have grown. Growth demands that you do a new job, one designed to handle the increased growth and demands.

If you say, "Hey, this doesn't apply to me. I don't have a start-up business." You would be right and wrong at the same time. Right in that you probably don't have a start-up. Wrong in that it applies to you if you want to grow your business.

Every type of business has its choke points, unique factors, and different sets of jobs that occur at different levels of productivity or sales.

A CEO of a micro business of one million dollars in annual revenue has different demands and duties than one that has grown to five million. This is logical. Not hard to agree, is it?!

The choke points for the growing company's CEO are mindset limitation and doing what he has always done. Usually he was so integral in every facet of his practice or business that the ability to scale the business drops away. He becomes the limiting factor. Unaware that he has a new job that invariably occurs with growth, he continues to do the old one. The result is a company or practice that falls back to the span of control to which he is accustomed! He is angry, often vowing to never grow again; it was just too much stress.

It was stress, all right. But that stress did not come from afar. It came from continuing to do what he had always done, expecting it to continue to be successful based on past experience. Seems reasonable. When it wasn't, he worked longer hours. Tried harder. Micromanaged more. The stress only worsened. There just wasn't enough of him to go around to do all the work he used to do. His job and its demands had changed and he had not.

This is a predictable situation. Some CEOs, which includes you if you have a small business or professional practice, do grow beyond their former thinking and emerge as capable leaders of the new growing company.

Sadly, too few do and become stuck or worse.

It IS more than a little counter-intuitive to realize that your job as you grow is to work yourself out of all the jobs you do. Yet, that is the truth. Leadership demands for a professional practice with three to five employees is quite different when the team has grown to twice that number. Every doubling of employees puts new demands on your systems of personnel hiring, training, and management. Having ten is quite different than having thirty-six. Ask me how I know.

In every key facet of your business, growth demands growth on your part.

It is just plain smart to grow yourself and your skill sets before the demand is there. Not remarkably, the acquisition of these skills helps to propel your business to the very heights to which you aspire.

Leaders matter. No matter where you look, a competent leader can make the difference between a roaring success and a flop. It isn't easy. But, if it was, everyone would be a competent leader or CEO. Well, we know that isn't true.

So what are you to do?

Here are some suggested principles for you to consider:

* Accept the nature of your job. As you grow, you actually take on a new job. Stop doing the old job expecting a different result.
* Commit to self-development and skill building before you actually need them. This demands that you accept the role of the lifelong learner.
* Innovate. The search for new, more, better, easier, faster never ends. Accept this and thrive.
* Deny it and get swept by, rolled over, or made simply inconsequential.
* Every person in an organization should accept the fact that if he is to ascend in the organization, he must increase his abilities, demonstrate competence, and get the desired results. (This includes you!)
* If you keep doing what you have always been doing as you grow, your company will, at best, struggle; at worst, begin to fail. Often, this means the company will slide back to your level of competence as a Leader CEO. (If you were in a larger company that you did not control, you would be fired. Rightfully so.)
* The more growth that occurs, the more you need reports, numbers, and measurements that detail what is going right and what is going not so right. Your need for result reporting grows. You cannot manage by gut or how it feels. You simply can't be everywhere.
* Evolve your systems to match your growth. Systems that worked at one level can be hopeless at higher levels. Often

these show up in IT and your systems of working with people.

* As the company grows, work to delegate every job you can. Often these are sales, marketing, engineering, and science related.
* You becoming more technically competent in your area of expertise has less and less effect as you grow. Often, many small business owners and professionals continue to increase their technical prowess as some sort of substitute for working on self-development and leadership. This is almost never the missing ingredient once sufficient technical competence is attained.
* Make decisions faster and insist that your people do as they promised they would. Hold people to the standards you have set.
* Accept that you may have to do micromanagement and be ready to do so, but only briefly.
* Replace those that keep dragging you into the jobs they should do. Stop tolerating incompetence. Dismiss the person you know should go. Insist on performance.
* Focus on the values, vision, purposes, business why, goals, and strategy. Think big and have your team step up to fill in the missing details. Live what you believe.
* Communicate more. Bring your people "in" by sharing information they need to engage and buy-in. Don't worry about being inspirational. Your passion for your purpose will do that just fine.
* Get help if needed, to grow yourself and your business, from a competent coach. (Yeah, that is a bit self-serving, but, nevertheless, true.)

If you are happy as a business or practice owner with your current state of growth, simply continue what you have been doing.

But if you want more...

Grow yourself and take on the larger leadership role BEFORE you must. Think ahead. Plan ahead. Learn ahead. Become the CEO that would need to exist for the level of growth you want. Then admire how fast that growth occurs. Your choice.

How do you choose?

Rhythms, Dead Spots, and Discipline

Virtually every day I see them pour through. Hundreds of them. Emails. Good golly, Miss Molly. Where do entrepreneurs and practice owners get the time to chat online and send endless emails?!

I observe these when I have self-assigned times to check emails. But some of these entrepreneurs, doctors, and small business people in various groups seem to have no other work to do. Long outpourings come forth. Champions for one concept or another demand that others accept their viewpoints. Arguments occur. Wasted time and effort over nuance and unimportant things. Silly.

Occasionally, a pearl of knowledge comes through which is the only thing that keeps me paying any attention at all.

If these full-on email and message board "players" are spending so much time online, what does it say about their business or professional practice? Who has the time for this?

Every successful entity has unyielding requirements for productive work. The one element all have in common is time to do that work. All have the same amount.

How you manage your time controls an enormous chunk of your success. So you can rapidly understand my consternation with those who waste my time and their own.

When I look to work with someone, how they manage their time tells me a great deal about them. The "always available to anyone" can't be that way without neglecting their own business or professional practice in some way, usually in a way that robs them of a huge chunk of their profits.

So how does one manage one's time successfully? Entire books have been written—hundreds of them. You may have read a few. Instead, here are simple and powerful axioms. Nothing complicated. Just solid 1-2-3 principles you can adopt and apply.

So what are these three principles?

* Prioritize
* Schedule
* Use the Dead Spots

Hold on. That seems too simple, you say. Well, it may be simple but you can remember it and apply it. These principles practiced get results. Why not just try these on for size? Chances are they are tailor-made for you.

Prioritize

You would think that this would be the easiest—but apparently it is the hardest.

When you can name what you want, life gets easier by quantum leaps. Then it becomes a matter of keeping these in mind and prioritizing your time based on what you want.

The trick seems to be that most people never really claim their preferred future because they never decide what they want. A secondary reason seems that new goals need to be set because the earlier ones were accomplished. I see this happen with professionals all the time. Successful entrepreneurs likewise suffer this when they reach their targets of business success or have an equity event where they sell. Some call this period "resting." The only problem is resting too long. Without a course set, you can wander around aimlessly.

Decide what you want. Take aim. Prioritize what is the most important and spend time there. Just be sure to include all parts of your life in your priorities. Otherwise, parts—important parts—will get neglected.

So once your priorities are straight, what do you do?

Schedule

Assign times for your activities and stick to the time assigned with the very, very rare exceptions. Simple. Doing this is the trick because (1) so many people never prioritize what is important, and (2) so many allow themselves to be moved by the seemingly urgent and neglecting the important.

Literally assign times for your activities. Best if done for all activities, but as a bare minimum within your practice or business.

Counter-intuitively, forcing time to your desired use gives you more freedom and keeps you on course. Say what?!

Scheduling your time within your business means to assign times for daily, weekly, monthly, quarterly and annual actions, meetings, and reviews. Doing this creates a sort of rhythm that assures that all the importances are covered. (Rhythm is a word I first heard used by Verne Harnish of Gazelles. It is a good word because, like music, a good rhythm can help carry you and your business to "hit" status.)

Beware of the little voice inside you that can rear its head and say some variant of "Who has the time for this!" Quiet that naysaying voice and here's why: the most successful create these rhythms of actions, meetings, and reviews. And stick to them. It "buys" time and brings freedom. Just as a money budget has set-asides of incoming funds to make them available for known and normal expenditures, so too does management of a business entity require a budget of time with set-asides to be spent utilizing your attention, energy, efforts, and smarts on all the various aspects of your business.

Three other strong reasons to implement these rhythms: these remove the angst of incompletions that gnaw at your sense of satisfaction, remove the uneasy feeling of "I should be doing more," and remove the omissions that invariably occur when these rhythms are missing. The net-net-net result is a stronger, more prosperous business or practice.

What about those dead spots that drop unexpectedly into your day? Those times when you are supposed to be doing x, but something or someone changed it so that previously scheduled time is "empty." I call these unexpected times dead spots. Why? Because for the vast majority, these are dead in regard to productive use of your time or others.

So what do most do with these dead spots? They talk to their co-workers, or check emails or post tweets or make a Facebook post. Zero productive work. The reality is that chatting it up with your co-workers kills your time and theirs! Thus the name: dead spot. No productive work. Remember the only thing that is unbuyable is time. How you use it should be done based on conscious decision, not the unconscious decision to somehow fill your time with the inane.

Of course, if you are consciously choosing to spend your dead spots with some form of socialization off-course from the purpose of your business or practice, and if it is a choice made with full awareness, have at it.

Here is a question for you: would you want your team members to do this? I doubt it. You want them productive, getting their re-sults, efficiently, profitably, right? Why should you, of all people, set a bad example?

How can you, with a good conscience, neglect your duties during these dead spots and ask your team members not to do as you do?

You have rights and responsibilities to lead, guide, and manage your group for success. Be the leader they and your clients want and deserve.

So how does one manage these dead spots and turn these snippets of time to advantage?

* Realize these happen and work to make them as minimal as possible. If you have a lot, it is time to take an honest appraisal of the business or practice activities and rhythms.
* Have a list of actions to be completed in your day, priori-tized, of course. With a dead spot, start down your list, matching the time snippet available to the priority at hand.
* Use the time to communicate to existing or potential new clients with personal notes, follow-ups, calls, and even emails. Relationships are important and can mean the dif-ference between screaming success and mediocre meander-ings that yield limp along, "just managing to exist" practices or businesses.
* Go acknowledge or thank your individual team members. This is the soul sustenance they require—we all require. Feed this need with ample portions to the deserving.

* Review reports and progress in accomplishing your targets. Make course corrections as needed. Consider where you are.
* Inspect your business or practice. Go with eyes wide open, taking the viewpoint of clients or patients. Notice what is going right and not. Speak to your team. If your business exists in the digital world, inspect your websites for ease of use, intuitive sense, and feeling created by its design. Check on your customer support. Send out a quick survey to clients to solicit feedback on what is going right and what needs help.
* Knowingly take a break for five minutes. (Not twenty.) Yep, you can do that too. Just remember that if this is the default use of the dead spots, you are either dull or unknowing or don't really care.

This is certainly not an all-inclusive list. These are the barest bones of a successful time used skeleton, but, if done, you are well on your way.

A final word: doing this takes a certain discipline. This is the discipline of the successful. This is the road to results. Simple, but not always easy.

How successful do you really want to be?

How You Live

How Fumbling for My Keys Led Me to a Profound Life Lesson

Sometimes the smallest things in life have the most significant impact for learning. A few years ago, I was getting out of my car to go into my office. I thought I should pick up a few things and take them in with me. Soon I had my briefcase, my laptop, my power cord, assorted trash, and an empty bottle of water.

My hands were full—too full. I walked to the backdoor to my office. Now I had to get to my keys to open up the door. You guessed it. I didn't have enough hands to handle all the items. Things started falling out of my hands. Crap! I had to remember I had my laptop in my hands so I didn't drop that.

I looked for a place to put something down just to organize myself for the moment. There wasn't one! Curse word, curse word, I muttered to myself. The great thing about the term "curse word" is its utility and broad use anywhere you are to let others know the intensity of your present thought or feeling.

Finally I managed to arrange the excessive load of items and unlock my door and get inside. Physically I only have two hands.

That means I can handle only so many items in those hands at one time. Too many and something gets dropped, accidents happen.

Mentally, there is an equivalent to the physical two hands. This means that you can only concentrate on so many things at once without feeling overwhelmed or hearing yourself say, "How can I possibly get all these things done?!" Some people see themselves weighed down by having so much going on at once. There is a solution.

Peter Drucker said that managers can only handle or oversee five people at a time. He went on to say that for some above average people, this number could go to seven or, in very exceptional cases, nine. For less capable mortals, only three.

Trying to do too much at once prevents you from getting what you want and frustrates your sense of completion. Only you can determine your span of concentration. You are far better off concentrating on fewer things and getting them done well than to have a slew of projects all going on at once. You should look at your history of getting things done and get a feel for what makes sense for you. In this case, do listen to that inner voice that knows the answer.

Once you know your span of concentration comfort level, limit your active projects to that number. Concentrate all your efforts to just those. Any additional ones get put on a list and get prioritized. This is one workable solution. The problem with this methodology is that it limits how much and how fast you get things done—because it is all up to you.

A better solution is to leverage your time. How? Delegate the projects to your team based on project priority, existing workload and talent of team members. This could double, triple, or quadruple the speed of your accomplishments. It is far better to supervise three to five team members with one to two projects each than to do it all yourself. Plus, you get to coach and teach your team members as you go along. This makes projects easier and faster to get done. Sure, you can still take on a project, but only if you choose to do so.

I seriously doubt you need more to do. The truth is that I want you doing less, working smarter, supervising more. Leverage and delegation of efforts is part of the formula for more success with less effort.

Here is a 1-2-3 quick summary:

* Know your own span of concentration (3-5-7-9 projects at a time). Go for less to begin with if this concept is new to you.
* Prioritize your projects and do list. Make this your standard operating procedure.
* Delegate more with your supervision and coaching.

Most of your team wants to help. Beware of those who shirk taking on more when asked, unless he or she already has a big workload. If you do these, you will see the difference, feel better at the end of the day, and hear your team talk excitedly about what they have accomplished together.

Review, Renew, and Refocus

Ahaaa, the end of the year holidays…the time to eat too much, be polite to extended family you haven't seen all year, and spend too much on gifts. It is also the time to count our blessings, remember those we love, and to bask in the warmth of relationships renewed.

How you view it is a matter of the perspective you take. For you, I hope it is a joyful time. If nothing else, this is the time of year to enjoy a time out from the hustle and bustle of everyday life.

(Although for some, it is a far more hectic time of year, including moms who are coordinating families and the "whole holiday thing" nearly single-handedly.)

It is also a time to collect your thoughts, take a look back at the year that just passed, and congratulate yourself for the successes in your life. Success comes in many forms and only you can define the form that is true for you. It is important to define what success will look like, otherwise you can spend a lifetime searching for elusive success that you never defined. So define it you must.

Once defined, it can be a lot like finding your way to a new place on roads untraveled. You can make the wrong turn or find yourself at a dead end. Then the only sensible thing to do is to retrace your steps. It might not feel good to have to backtrack, but such is the way of life. Often it takes a couple of steps back before you can go five steps forward.

I trust you find that the holidays, among other times, are a time of personal rest and renewal that gives birth to new energy, new creativity, and refocusing on the things that are important to you. It is a time for reflection and planning your future as well.

Let's get practical for a moment. Here are ten steps to complete the year and prepare for what you want to accomplish in the next year. I suggest you take these steps to heart if you want to see your successes leap forward into a whole new realm.

* Review your accomplishments for the year. Make a list. How do you feel about the year? What do you hear yourself saying about how it went? Is the picture of the year just past one you are proud to have created?
* List out the targets that you have not reached yet.
* Decide which ones are worth continuing.

* Throw out the rest that don't meet your definitions of successes.
* Make a new list of goals to accomplish. Include all areas of your life, not just your practice/ business.
* Make a list of current activities. Throw out the ones that no longer apply or de-emphasize those that aren't as important as others. You may remember these as your Don't Do List.
* Plan out what is important to you. Delegate as much as pos-sible. It isn't right or fair for you to have to bear the entire load. Remember to plan out the time, finance, authority, and who will get the goal/project accomplished. It will take longer to get individual projects done to your satisfaction, but you'll get more of them done without wearing you out by leveraging your team.
* Implement the projects/goals/do list. Usually, one at a time for team members, and no more than three at a time for the entrepreneur, manager, or director. If you have an as-sociate or junior, use him to get projects done - it is just part of the working arrangement. It will often take twice as long to get a project done than one would normally expect. Expect this.
* Set deadlines for completion, realizing that your team will have to complete these on top of what they are already do-ing. Measure project steps by due date. Often a project will require changes from the original plan to complete as les-sons are learned. Therefore, all projects are written up as pilots, subject to change. It is still a team effort and each project is headed up by you, a direct report, or team mem-ber as assigned or accepted. Look at your job as head coach, leading, guiding, and teaching.

* Celebrate the successes. Give high achievers more to complete and reward them for doing so. Give financial, social, and moral incentives for success. Recognize publicly. Modify projects as needed to suit your needs.

Remember there will be the pressure of the urgent to not get these important projects done. You have to see the value long-term and the consequences of not getting these done.

The first six steps you can complete alone. Do this as soon as possible. Set aside some time, whatever is necessary, for you to think through these steps. Put yourself in the environment where you think the best and give yourself a reward for completing steps one through six.

I suggest that you go over the business-related plans for the year with your team at the annual planning meeting held early in the year. This meeting helps put your team "in the know" and propels your business forward far faster than not having the annual planning meeting, which is the norm for too many.

By the way, whenever things have seemed to go awry, this end of the year plan can be invoked at any time of the year. The process can get back on track as well as keep you on track.

Stress and the Big Lesson from the Great Barrier Reef

There are many ways to handle stress. The important thing is to not let it get to you. If you are one of these chronically stressed people, here is one thing you can do:

Expect It.

Huh? Yeah. That's right. Expect it. Accept it as part of living. Life is full of surprises that one can't control. Get used to it. Fortunately, those aren't the main sources of most folks' excessive stress.

What is the main source? An unreasonable expectation that life can and should be simple and relaxed. It is not.

The Great Barrier Reef off the northeast coast of Australia is teeming with life, full of all manners of plant and animal life. It is home to the great white shark and some of the most beautiful species in all the oceans. But wait.

Not all is idyllic here. The water here is rough, difficult; the underwater terrain treacherous. Not far away is another area where the waters are placid. Calm. Peaceful. The terrain a sand bottom. But the sea life is dull, certainly not colorful. The number of species fewer. But it looks to the unobservant to be the more desirable of the two.

Your business and your life are certainly similar to these two vastly different environments. If you choose the rough water of life, you choose to participate, to be an active player who understands that if you want to really play, one must accept that the water is rough and learn to enjoy the thrills, chills, and spills of living. The rough water is part of life. It can't be ignored or discounted or not accepted for what it is.

The other choice is to continually reject and be upset with it. This is silly. Life's vicissitudes are a lot like gravity. You can reject it, but still the object falls to the earth every time. Count on life to have rough waters as much as you can count on gravity to bring objects back to earth.

A case in point, my wife and I have a large house: three floors and seven bedrooms. When all of our five children were home and growing up, the place could get rough, lots of noise, activity and often arguments and bickering back and forth among the children. To this day, I still don't enjoy the fights over who wore whose clothes! But it was full of life, activity, energy, and joy.

Now all five children have left home, it is much quieter. Less full of life. My wife, one day, had the realization that she liked it better the other way. She said, "It's too quiet."

Too little activity is more dangerous to one's health and happiness than too much. Now, when the children come home, they are welcomed. Don't tell my kids, but I would rather have the bickering and the laughing than the quiet and relatively placid environment of their absence! Yes, home life is "rougher," but a lot more fun.

Your business is much the same way. You either create the specific stressors you want to have— the good problems. Or you let your business dictate its problems to you. You become reactive, on the defensive, rejecting the problems as if someone else was responsible for their creation.

A case in point: would you rather have too few patients or deal with the problem of too many! Look at all the choices you have when you have too many. You could learn to become faster, more efficient. Raise your fees or prices. Stop feeling needy and increase your choices of what you want to do. When people are clamoring for appointments with you, life is good.

When you have too few, you become needy, forcing a "I must have a yes" to a presented offering (which always works against you financially and emotionally.) You get bored because you aren't as busy as you would like. The problem of too much is generally easier to handle than too little. Get busy and create the right kind of problems.

A Personal Setback and Some Personal Epiphanies

There it was and it wasn't going away. Still, I was hoping it would. It was there since 6:30 this morning and it was now 6:30 in the evening. Crap. I made the call to my physician. As luck would have it, he wasn't on call. I got my orders from the on-call physician. "Go to the emergency room right now," came the command flying out of her mouth at supersonic speed.

Crap and more crap.

I told my wife I was going, but not to worry, it probably wasn't anything. I knew I had to go and hoped it wasn't really anything to worry about—even then knowing I was kidding myself. As soon as I hit the emergency room door and said the words "chest pain," I was ushered into a triage area without even giving my name. It took ten minutes into the visit before anyone asked for my name or my insurance card. It was now 7:30 PM.

At 11:00 PM, I learned it wasn't my heart. Whew. Still I was in pain. The ER doc said it had to be something because of its nature, too much pain to dismiss as indigestion. The symptoms pointed another direction.

"It could be a PE," he mused as he looked mentally into his data banks. He paused for more than a few seconds. "We need to do a CAT scan of your legs and chest." Now, he was surer, though still searching for the diagnosis.

My answer to him was, "What is a PE?" I felt I should have known the lingo for whatever a PE was, but I wasn't going to let this stop me from knowing.

"Pulmonary embolism," he responded just as quickly. Crap again.

Two hours later, after the CAT scan and more blood studies and yet another EKG, came the confirmation of a pulmonary embolism in my left lower lobe of my lungs. No wonder my chest hurt so badly. I also had a clot in the popliteal vein behind my left knee.

"This isn't supposed to happening to me. I work out. I am healthy," I thought silently.

"We'll have to admit you. You'll be here at least for five days," the ER doc pronounced with finality.

Grudgingly, I nodded in agreement. At 2 AM Sunday morning, I was placed in a small private room and started on anticoagulant therapy. I stayed until Friday to get my therapeutic clotting level down to twice the normal level. That was a lot of time to just lay there. Boy, I hate doing nothing at all. So I got busy with what I could do.

I read. I researched. It also gave me time to think. I came to some realizations. Those realizations I want to share—at least some of them. Here are three.

* You will become what you think about and what you talk about most. The language you speak to yourself colors and

filters everything into and out of your world. Pissing and moaning about your problems does nothing because you have put the cause of your problems over somewhere else, where you can do nothing about them. You are the effect. This is the essence of being a victim. · There is a natural law, as sure as the sun rising each day, that if all you do is piss and moan, you will get more of the same kind of problems. Blame doesn't get results; doing something about the problem does.

* Life and practice is full of ups and downs. I don't care how great a person you are or how great a leader, entrepreneur, manager, or director you are, problems will come up. This is just a fact of life AND you are equipped to handle it. Things will turn up, get better if you keep doing the right things and actively keep the faith in yourself and all that you are.
* Success takes work.

"The only place where success comes before work is in the dictionary."
- Vidal Sassoon

The reality is that if you want to be the one in twenty that achieves real success, then you have probably worked harder at it than 95 percent of the people who said they wanted it but chose not to work at it.

Of course, we all want to work smarter and not harder, and certainly my program leverages your time and money to get you there faster. Still, it is the willingness to do, to act that separates you from the other 95 percent.

Ideas are everywhere. What you do with them makes all the difference.

I had four months of this therapy to endure, but it sure beats the alternative. I had quite a few more realizations. I will save those for another time.

I leave you with this quote—wisdom from another time not too long ago.

"How far you go in life depends on your being tender with the young, compassionate with the aged, sympathetic with the striving and tolerant of the weak and strong. Because, someday in life you will have been all of these."
-George Washington Carver

Ups and Downs

It happens to everybody…but, if you know what to do, it is infinitely easier to deal with and prevent for the future.

The thing that happens is that you outrun your schedule. You have a big month and then a little month, then a big month and then a little month, over and over. This is a signal of big trouble looming. The big trouble is that you can't plan or anticipate production and income. It is a sure way to have significant cash flow problems.

These ups and downs are an indicator of a lack of organization. When the month is down, you have time to work on marketing and selling as well as all the other parts of making your business sing.

Your efforts pay off with a visible upswing in productivity. This upswing can come in as little as two weeks, but more likely six weeks. So now you are busy delivering your products and services. So what is the problem? You are too busy to do the things that got you productive in the first place!

New case consults are fewer as there is just too little time to get them done. Marketing efforts fall off. You are so busy in the now that you fail to plan and make your future.

This pattern will repeat itself over and over. The difficulty is planning for personnel, expenditures, time to train, office work, etc. It is a feast or famine. A statistician could say you're fine if you just average the two. As Lee Corso of ESPN fame would say, "Not so fast my friend." This vicious cycle can eat your profits.

So what do you do to handle this vicious cycle?

You can do as my dear departed father-in-law used to do. He was a builder, subject to up and down cycles in the building construction industry. When times were good, he would save and build up reserves. He did not add capacity, personnel, equipment, etc. When the boom slowed down, he would count on his reserves to provide a smooth continuous flow of income. It worked for him. This may be the solution you should use.

The problem with the solution is that he permanently capped how far his business could grow. He built it for lean times. He couldn't take advantage of the booms because he limited his capacity. He missed out on oodles of projects that could have paid him handsomely at the time. He didn't have a real marketing effort; it was all word of mouth. He never organized his business beyond what he himself could take on. These concepts of organization and marketing weren't foreign to him. He just didn't see himself as being more than a small builder and he didn't want the "hassle and headaches" of growth. He chose a lifestyle that fit his income and was fairly content with it.

He also was tied to his business. He couldn't leave it. He limited his income. He could have been a multi-millionaire. He never took those trips that he and my mother-in-law had always talked about. His health deteriorated. He retired. A few years later my mother-in-law died from breast cancer. A few years after that, he died from complications of lung cancer—70 years young. I miss my in-laws; they were good, loving people who raised six kids well.

So what is the other choice? Delegate your work so you can concentrate on only leading, planning, marketing your business, and doing your—a simple answer with a more complex implementation.

Here's a starting point. Figure all that you do. Make a complete list. Make a rough guess of time you put into each area. Immediately delegate any and all activities that someone else can do without a significant amount of time training them to do it. If there are actions you like to do because you enjoy them, fine, do them. Just realize that doing so takes away from other activities that may be more profitable financially. Take your list and prepare materials and training so that someone else can take over the more challenging actions. This can take quite a bit of time.

Not doing this is asking for an unending enslavement to tasks, activities, and jobs that limit your productivity, income, and time off.

Yes, it is a lot of work. Yes, it will take a lot of time. Yes, it will be a challenge. And it is so worth it in the end.

Think and plan more, but do less. Here's to you doing what you do best.

Being Real

It was the end of the day and I was seeing a long-time patient, Joe, a retired oil company exec, to complete some dental work.

He asked me, "Charley, how are you?" in the normal good manners and social graces kind of way. I surprised him a bit when I said, "Stressed!"

He immediately responded with, "Gee, I understand why. You have been seeing patients all day and you are probably tired?"

I replied, "No, Joe, that's not it. I have a daughter getting married next Saturday and my wife is stressed out. So I am stressed out, too."

Joe reflected a moment and then chuckled. "Oh, Charley, I understand. Congratulations. I can certainly understand how you'd be stressed."

"Thanks, Joe," I swiftly answered.

"Anything I can do?" he responded genuinely.

"No, except help me out a little bit here. I have a haircut appointment in twenty minutes that I have to keep or my wife will kill me. I am going to be finishing off with you a little more quickly than usual."

"Sure. No problem," Joe quickly agreed.

Usually Joe and I had a little talk each time we visited, discussing the events of the day or local politics. We both looked forward to these chats. I knew Joe would have felt a little hurt if I didn't explain my need to abbreviate our chat.

I could sense Joe's satisfaction in contributing to my schedule. It is amazing what you can pick up from another without him even saying anything more.

As luck and typical schedules have it, I still wasn't out of the woods yet. A new patient had come in before Joe. He was still there when Joe came in. This was an eighty-three-year-old MIT chemical engineer with the gift of gab. He owned his own company and was still active as its CEO. He was an inventor, entrepreneur, and salesman all lumped together in a fascinating package of humankind. I really liked him.

As you can probably imagine, his medical condition and mouth condition were such that he needed a lot of medical history review, dental history review, and oral diagnosis. I had to get on the phone to his physician while he was still in my chair. I completed the oral exam. His mouth was a mess.

He went by his first two initials: T. C. "T. C., you have a challenging situation," I started.

"I very well know that," he interrupted gently. "That's why I came to you. I researched you very thoroughly before I ever made an appointment. I know you can take care of me."

I had no real idea how he had done his research other than online, but I rather liked his conclusion.

"T. C., I will need more information still yet to diagnose you properly and to figure out your best treatment."

He nodded in agreement.

"But, I have a problem. My daughter, Kelley, is getting married next Saturday and if I don't get my haircut my wife is going to kill me. My appointment is in ten minutes. I am going to leave you with my team to gather the remaining records. Is that OK with you?"

He smiled knowingly. "A wedding, huh. I understand perfectly. Doc, it is fine. Go ahead and I'll see you later. I certainly want to take care of the person who is taking care of me."

"Thank you for your help and understanding," I replied, relieved and feeling less stressed already. My team gathered the remaining records while I scooted out the door to my haircut.

So what is the take home pay for you out of this? People like to help and if you communicate with them genuinely they respond in ways that can sometimes amaze you—even when you don't know them that well. My long time patient Joe was more likely to be understanding—and he was. T. C., on the other hand, might not have been so understanding. The key was my willingness to be real and let him know what was going on for me. Both could identify with my situation.

There is a rather open secret to all this. People like to contribute. They like to help. Why? The answer is because they feel better about themselves and like others to do well too.

Contribution, contributing, and being contributed to, is one of the joys of life. Here's to your joy.

The Myth of Staying the Same

It happened innocently…still she was a bit miffed. I didn't quite notice immediately.

I shouldn't have been surprised. She and her two teammates were in the top two percent of all the folks that answer the phone. They all took my recently made comments as unbridled criticism. I could see it in their faces. First one, then another and then the final one. Their facial expressions gave it away, although the first one to show her displeasure at my comments did nothing to conceal it.

I trudged on. I knew that the reaction needed addressing. I ignored it for the time because I was intent on solving an inconsistency in how we answered the phone.

So we went through the sequences for answering the phone. I sent the front desk team out of the team meeting to create a simple one-page flow chart of how calls are supposed to be answered, while giving the other team members time to work on their performance-based job descriptions.

To their credit, they took the assignment and quickly came back with a very workable flow chart. Not only that, they did not dwell in the land of "Poor ol' me. He is picking on us and he shouldn't be. We do the best we can." No, they were more mature than that.

We went over the entire sequence in the flow chart, delving into the details that were part and parcel of each step. The entire team perked up, as the details indicated where the inconsistencies were showing up. Even the assistants and hygienists were all ears.

The flow chart gave all of us a picture.

Then the stuck point could no longer be held back.

She blurted out, "We do the best we can." I believed her. Still that wasn't the point.

Even if you are doing the best you can, the moment you stop thinking there is more to learn and improve, you are already sliding backwards. When you continue to believe you can improve, and there is more to know, you will keep learning, propelling yourself upward. The moment you stop working to improve or think you have arrived is the moment you start to slide back. Even the very best succumb to the trap of thinking they are at the top of the heap and can rest on the past.

The universe is far more likely to say: what have you done lately? Look, my team are very, very good. So am I. However, the moment we "start believing our press clippings," we start the inevitable slide backwards. When we stop believing that getting better is possible, we are destined to slide backwards.

Once the slide has begun, the work to rectify the situation can be daunting. Why? It will take some time just to stop the downward fall. It is at this point that it is easy to succumb to the thought that the work to improve is failing. Au contraire. The reality is that it takes some time and continuing effort. You can't quit too soon.

A quick example. It takes eight to twelve weeks of working out to start to see any real change in weight for most folks over age 40. This is quite different from when we are younger. Yet, most people don't realize the physiologic change of normal aging and expect the working out to have near immediate effects like when we were in our twenties! I found this out the hard way. I worked out well for a solid six weeks without much change in weight at all. Discouragement City! I had stopped too soon, just before the breakthrough was about to occur. ARRRRGGH!

My team brightened up immediately when I explained the concept of continual improvement and what happens when you stop. The truth is that there is also an upward momentum generated after a while so that the effort gets easier and doesn't take as much energy. That's where you want to get.

It has been a principle for me for many years—I must continue to get better. I work to expand my strengths regularly—read a book a week, attend seminars and conferences forty to fifty days a year, work with the best around, digest many magazines and periodicals monthly, comb through Internet updates, listen to educational CDs, participate in mastermind groups, and lead groups of my own. It is all just part of what I do.

The best never stop getting better, more educated, more polished, more able, more knowledgeable, and more skilled.

This can be viewed as one of life's enjoyments, or as the curse of the universe. You get to choose.

How You Market

Firewalls, City Walls, and Mental Walls

The Secrets to Getting Your Clients to Let You In

My computer blinks its message each time I fire it up. "Your firewall is on." My digital existence feels protected from unwanted, potentially destructive intruders who have no business inside my hard drive, executing programs that take valuable data away from me or have it do someone else's digital bidding, or worse, causing a hard drive meltdown. There. I feel better.

Protection has been sought through the ages. The old cities of Europe were built on hills with three to sixteen foot thick walls. The remnants of these walls still exist in the modern cities built around, over, and through them.

Man has always sought safety and refuge from the unwanted invaders, pirates, and enemies of the state behind physical walls that prevent them from entering. These "walls" were often moats, mountains, and sheer distance. Armies would march out to create a human wall between an enemy and a city. Navies created a sea-based blockade "wall" to throw back attackers from foreign lands.

Today the invasions are on a whole new plane that did not exist in the old world—it is the invasion of communication.

Your prospect faces an avalanche of marketing armies coming at him, each marketing soldier wanting to extract money or time or energy or votes. These come from all angles through an increasing variety of communication media and channels. A new wave arrives each day.

Some marketing soldiers (messages) get through to create effects. Most are beaten back.

The marketers' response to this resistance has been to "pile it on," literally to put out more marketing messages, to increase the number of channels and how much goes into each one. The idea is that if enough are put out there, some are bound to get through.

The prospect's response has been to ignore more. Particularly galling marketing messages get legislated out of existence by a Congress that listens to its constituents, hence, the ban on spam, unsolicited faxes, and telemarketers' calls into the home.

The marketer has tried to become inventive, creating unusual, memorable and, most often, failing campaigns. You may remember the Taco Bell's talking dog? You remember the dog, but the only thing that the executives remember is the decrease in sales! A miserable failure by trying to be cute, entertaining, and attention-getting (all good), without an underlying connection to the offering.

Do you know of anyone saying, "More marketing, please?"

What goes unrecognized is what happens to the cognitive and creative capacity of individuals when one's mind is inundated with all the marketing messages. It gets overwhelmed. In computer-speak, there isn't enough bandwidth to handle it all. The mind shuts down just like a computer that can't process everything. This is not a pleasant state. So what are your prospective patients doing about it?

They are relying on some form of mental wall to fend off the messages, to protect the bastion of their pocketbook and reclaim some sanity in the din of marketing noise.

It is not as if every marketing message is unwanted—many are wanted. So rather than creating a solid wall, the mental one is full of holes called T.T.I.M. (pronounced Tim) "things that interest me." T.T.I.M. is composed of problems needing solving, individual needs, wants, and personal interests.

It is not a solid wall. Think of it more like a filter. Your prospect designs his filter so that what is important to him gets through.

In fact, you and your prospect operate the same way in this regard, you actually, gulp, dare I say, search out the areas of interest. It is an active wall that sends out its own feelers through its T.T.I.M. portals looking for offerings that solve the problems, answer the needs, feed the wants, and listen for the items of personal interest.

I use the term feelers for a special reason: your prospective patient is looking to find offerings that have benefits that make him feel better, healthier, richer, thinner, better looking, younger, admired. Literally, he is looking for the offerings that sing to his human emotions with the melody that sticks in his mind. The stickier you can make your offering, the easier it is to market.

The person and his personal wall feelers search the Internet, scour the airwaves, peruse the magazines and newspapers for solutions that bring meaningful results, solve problems, and help him feel better about himself and his world.

The Birth of Pull Marketing and the Rising Abhorrence to Push Marketing

Virtually all of your prospects are looking for offerings to buy. They want to buy. And it is a good thing they do, because they hate being sold. They have been abused so long that one could call this the Age of Skepticism. This skepticism is a huge wall of its own accord and has become culturally embedded in our society.

Overcoming this skepticism is now the second most important thing for your marketing intention and messages. (The first is getting attention in the first place.) Now the skepticism is rising because of the continuing attempt to overpower any resistance—literally pushing harder—to sell an offering, rather than make it a wanted one that people want to buy.

Even getting attention is getting harder because of marketers that lie to get attention in the court of the marketplace. The reality is that these lying marketers are, in actuality, marketing criminals. They don't know enough about how to present their messages effectively so instead they do most anything to get your attentionand patronage. They push, mislead, and misguide for their own ends—and people hate them for it. Many more years of the present status will sway the public to look at marketing through the same jaundiced eye as the used car salesman. Yeech.

If you take a look, you'll see that the public is beginning to paint the entire field of marketing with the brush formed in the crucible of past history from these despicable characters. The bitter emotional aftertaste of unethical marketing makes it harder for the ethical marketer to get his message across and cripples many right-minded attempts to serve the public. Simply put, bad marketing by some makes marketing harder for the good guys.

Your job is to market effectively, in spite of the marketing mistrust, and set a good marketing example. So how do you do that?

Push and I Resist, Attract and I'll Pull Myself In

So how do you attract your client?

How do you become chocolate for the chocoholic?

How do you and your offerings become the magnet of irresistible force?

How can you become like gravity that always moves your prospect toward you, putting him in orbit around your planet?

Three Principles of Attracting and Working with Your Desired Client

* Appeal to Human Nature This sounds simple, but ultimately can be a difficult task. When offering a very good deal (cheap) on an offering, you cannot say, "You'll like this because it meets your greed need!" No, you must give reasons why you can offer it at such a good deal and point out

comparisons that are easily digested, leading your prospect to the inescapable conclusion that not buying is to miss out on something that is not to be missed!

So, the art of involving human nature and emotions requires a subtlety that repeatedly returns to the core message, preferably multiple times or, if done adroitly, that once is enough. The skilled writer does this so smoothly that nary a ripple occurs in your mind as his persuasion poker stirs your fire to buy to a roaring flame.

Some of the most successful influencers, leaders, speakers, and writers through the ages have used the power of story to capture the essential human essences to sway the audience to a specific point of view. Religious parables, folk tales of yore, urban legends (modern day versions of folk stories) use the power of story to get a message across and have it stick.

* Choose a Client Worth Having

Not every potential patient should be yours. Some are extremely valuable, providing you the professional satisfaction of helping your patient meet and conquer his challenges and doing it very profitably for both of you. He recognizes the contribution you make and gratefully acknowledges it.

Some drain your time, whine, complain, and make you the reason for their failure, and pat themselves on the back for their success, ignoring your contribution. Many of these patients cost you, not only emotionally, but also financially—you lose money on them. Many times, I have ad vised my clients to "fire" patients like this. The emotional relief of doing so may be more valuable than the money lost.

Here are some thoughts that you should keep in mind:

* What "good" are you doing for the patient whose mindset prevents you from doing your highest and best work?
* What effect does dealing with "the problem child" have on your ability to take good care of your best patients? Do you deliver a better or worse product, service, experience, or potential transformation?
* Do your best patients benefit from having bad ones in your fold?
* Do the tenacious tentacles of these sea monsters that try to drown you in their woe drain your creative energies?
* How much more profit could you make if you concentrated on your best patients and best prospective patients?
* Could it be that the problem patient would be better served by someone else who could mesh, deal with and serve your "pain in the backside" patient?

Concentrate on patients who allow you to help them successfully, that you can serve well, and that afford you a profitable experience, financially and emotionally. Then everyone wins. And isn't that what it is all about?

* Look from Outside In Virtually all dentists and entrepreneurs make the mistake of looking at the marketplace, clients, and opportunities from inside their own heads.

The smart operator looks from the point of view of the potential clients.

This is a never-ending challenge that requires a certain discipline, and often, others help. We all live inside our own heads, so it is only natural to use this point of view.

The key principle here is that you are not your patient. Your thinking comes from your thorough knowledge of your field, forever altering your ability to think like a newbie who does not see the breadth and depth of the value you bring.

What you see and hear and feel about your field where it all seems so simple is but a cloud of confusion for your unknowing neophyte, prospective patient. It is hard to appreciate what you do not understand well enough to value.

Your prospect values from inside his world, his interests, his problems, his frustrations, his aspirations, his dreams, and desires. He sees the world from inside his head.

Discover these and the path to gold and glory is clearly marked. How do you do this? Ah, that is the rub!

Seeing and hearing and feeling the world as your clients do leads to your understanding of how to provide your highest and best help.

So ASK!

Start by getting inside the heads of the best patients you currently have.

Find out about them — what are their frustrations, problems, cares, needs, interests, wants? What do they read, watch, listen to? What media do they use? What groups do they belong to or support? What do they like to do for fun? What do they value?

Then ask about your field. Ask them what they like and what they don't like. Ask them for their suggestions, ideas, and thoughts on improvements they rank as important.

It is amazing how little this is done even with simple paper and ink surveys. This is something everyone can do easily and inexpensively. Online surveys can be cheap and fast. Apply what you learn quickly and you will improve your business or practice overnight.

Surveys are not 100 percent reliable. Sometimes people don't want to tell you the entire truth because it is too revealing or they are concerned it would hurt your feelings. Sometimes they just don't know why they do what they do!

Look for commonalities among the answers; look for the theme presented by their answers. This can be applied to improve the sense of value you bring to your clients.

For a more in-depth probing, go oral. Interview your best patients. Help them understand they are helping you to do a better job, not just for them, but also potential patients you would like to have.

Ask the bigger questions and then sit back and listen with big ears, keep them talking and describing. The more they talk, the deeper they go. Listen for the essence of the messages. Listen for the between-the-lines "words" that aren't spoken.

Do not be surprised to have all types of emotions show up, including crying. Crying is good. Go with it and be sure to get it all talked out. Encourage the "going on and on" in their answers, for the further they go, the less self-censoring occurs and the more meat shows up.

The uncensored meat gives you the edge beyond the common everyday survey.

The result of all this interviewing and probing will be the emergence of a composite client—a persona whose personality and interests and needs are commonalities.

Usually it will be two to five of these personas that emerge for your practice. Oh, happy day when you find these because now you can address all your marketing messages to a "person" who is your best buyer or patient.

The result is a new level of resonance with the thinking, values, and feelings of those you most want. Now your marketing improves as it "speaks" more effectively to those you most want to reach. Results improve as you reach "the things that interest me" portals and feelers that seek you out.

Worry not about doing these things perfectly. You won't. It doesn't require perfection.

Just make progress.

An Entrepreneur's Biggest Mistake.

If it wasn't so obvious, it could be forgiven.

OK. I'll forgive it this once. But pay close attention so this whop-per doesn't get you. Let me illustrate with an example…

Larry has a small business that delivers health care. His practice has been ripping along now for a while - doing pretty well, thank you - until recently, when a huge drop-off whacked him unexpect-edly. New clients became sparse. Existing ones weren't coming in. Cash flow dried up. His paychecks became irregular. Payroll be-came a bimonthly drama—would he get enough money in to make those checks good? Larry figured he didn't need a sauna or steam; he could generate his own sweat of worry continuously.

When he contacted me for help, he was trying to keep his pro-fessional cool and not sound des- perate. He had that funny tone in his voice that belied his fear. He told me things had been going so well and suddenly went south. I went through my consultative interview designed to ferret out the main problems my clients face.

What was obvious to me, Larry was blind to see. Larry had managed to set his practice up in a fast-growing town when he had started out 15 years ago. Now that growth had cooled down to normalcy. Larry had been busy from day one of opening his doors. He had worked hard and was delivering his care well. He was doing OK in the money department—no great shakes, but well enough that his wife didn't nag him about the money he brought home, until now.

If anything, this was one of the more unsettling parts of the situation. He hated to let her down. Larry really was a bright guy, but like so many professionals and small business people, he was treating his practice more like a job than a business.

I asked Larry about his daily activities. He described them in great detail. His passion for his work plastered itself all over his words. The problem was that he couldn't cash a passion check. Larry was so busy working inside his practice that he had neglected marketing it. He knew he needed to; he was just so darn busy.

Naturally, he didn't think about what could happen if he didn't proactively ensure the steady flow of patients. He felt nearly over-whelmed already. When it hit him, he was simply unprepared.

Larry had marketed his practice some in the past. It was virtually all via the power of the pavement—he got out and walked around, met with associations, and got himself known in the community.

But since he had gotten so busy, he had stopped doing this himself and didn't have anyone else doing it either. Larry confided that he knew he should be doing something.

So have you figured out the mistake?

Marketing your practice or small business is a perpetual need.

If you neglect it or do it poorly, it will come back to bite you. Some businesses die from the bite, others take months or even years to recover.

Larry was a normal, intelligent guy with a love for his profession. He practiced at a high level. This used to be enough to be very good at what you do. It is not anymore.

Larry had stopped working to create his practice because he was busy working in it, providing services. It made him vulnerable and now he was paying the price in spades for omitting what he intuitively knew must happen.

Most people need a coach to help them see what they cannot. Larry later told me that just having a coach helped him "stay on his game."

We worked out how Larry could fix his problem. He swallowed hard when I told him all that would be necessary to get his market-ing ship righted and going full speed ahead. He accepted that it was going to take some time and no small sum of money to rectify the sins of his marketing omission.

Today Larry's marketing ship is under full sail and moving along with a fifteen mile an hour breeze. Larry, the marketing pilot, now keeps a smile on his face most of the time.

So what about you? Are you sailing along? Here are five principles for you:

Five "Keep it Going" Principles

* If you have a marketing program, make sure it is implemented consistently, on time, and systematically. Some business owners fall asleep at the marketing wheel regularly. It is scary. There ought to be a business and professions cop to give you a marketing ticket for failure to uphold your responsibility as a marketer, employer, and business owner, and placing employees and family at unnecessary risk. Sentence: the fine of worry, catch up marketing dollars, and an empty bank account.
* Track the results of your marketing efforts. Cut out the ones that are losers quick. If you have a successful campaign, keep doing what works. Unlike big business, you don't have millions to test what works. You can easily waste tens of thousands by marketing badly.
* You can't afford to test ultra-creative, "maybe will work" materials. You should use what is known to work to bring new clients and patients into your business or practice.

* Don't do what everyone else does and expect to get different results. This principle applies to virtually every aspect of your business.
* Deliver marketing messages that engage the mind and hearts of your prospective client. Talk about what is important to them and show them how your services, products, experiences, and transformations help them solve their problems.

Owning a business or practice, even in these different days, is a golden opportunity. This is the most affluent society the world has ever known. It can be a very good time…will it be for you?

The Seven Marketing Lessons of the Roman Coliseum

The Roman Coliseum, not just any coliseum, but the Coliseum, as the people of Rome call it, holds secrets to your success in marketing. How can that be?

It is an impressive structure, even today, after sixteen hundred plus years of abuse, rampage, theft of its very walls, invading hordes, and general neglect since the days when Rome was the power in the western world.

The Romans had a particular way they engineered walls that featured bricks laid length-wise, turned, and stacked in a diamond formation. How they came to know the durability of this weight-bearing design was lost when the Germanic tribes burned, buried, or destroyed anything Roman.

These were engineering masterpieces that silently boast of their resilience by still being there, when conventionally-built abodes, palaces, and streets have withered from time, use, and weather.

These Roman engineered edifices stand all over what was once the known civilized world.

The Coliseum itself has a series of columns, arches, walls, and portals on multiple levels. It could hold fifty thousand people for the events and games that became the amusement of the masses. It could disgorge its attendees in fifteen minutes.

There are seven important marketing keys from the Coliseum to remember and put into action. The Coliseum has multiple entrances to get inside. Each entry portal leads to a specific path to a specific section of the arena.

Your marketing should employ multiple portals (methods of marketing), too. Each marketing entrance should take your prospect down a specific marketing path based on the prospect's interest.

You can't depend on any one way to market your practice or business. The Law of One states that dependence on one of anything puts you and your business at unnecessary risk—one marketing method, one employee, one supplier, or one client. What happens if that "one" disappears, changes advisors, quits, or find another way that does not include you?

Multiple entrance portals give a diversity of getting new clients that ensures that even if one is taken away, you are safe. In fact, the dentist that relies on one way to get new patients into his practice puts himself at risk everyday.

I have watched previously successful businesses wither and die after legislation at the federal and state levels have killed broadcast faxes, outbound telemarketing, and the hated emails of the spam mongers.

Why put you and your business or practice at risk from too few marketing methods?

The Internet can be a particularly seductive marketing channel because it is generally cheap and fast. And remember this, what works today may be banned tomorrow if enough consumers get mad enough about it.

In investing, the smart investor diversifies and spreads the risk out among many different financial instruments. This way, if any one investment goes bad, the loss is capped and limited, while the other investments continue along their merry way making the investor money. Your marketing should do the same.

I have had many clients tell me that they prefer to let word of mouth and referrals supply them with all their new clients. This makes me very nervous for them. Why? I call this the Liability of Referral Dependence.

Now, avoid jumping to any conclusions quite yet. Let me explain. The key word is dependence. I like getting positive word of mouth and referrals as much as anyone. But there is a problem, Houston. It has to do with the passivity. Few are the systems for activation of positive word of mouth and active referral.

Most do not have a system at all. It is hope. The average practitioner has no control over it and merely waits and hopes that new patients are on their way. How's wait and hope as a strategy? Are you willing to turn your fate over to such?

You should have an active, thought-out design to your word of mouth and referral system. This is why I designed what I call the Optimum Referral Culture, which is an active system that you can control, and predictably yields new patients.

Hold on, there are two other reasons for diversity of marketing channels.

The first of these is multi-reach. Not every media reaches everyone. Each media type has its own advantages and should be used for those advantages. When you deploy multiple media, your message can reach more of your intended audience, and when done well, can lead to media synergy.

This is the synergy that occurs when your intended targets hear, see, or read about you and your offerings from multiple channels. Additively, these can tip the balance in your favor so that your prospect responds. A word of caution: you can diversify too widely and fail to use enough frequency to get "heard." Each media type must be deployed with enough frequency in that channel to create an effect.

Many dentists fall short here and waste their money because of it. You are better off reaching a smaller group multiple times than a far larger group once. You as a marketer need multiple ways to attract the clients you want.

Think like the builders of the Coliseum. The Coliseum had the first luxury boxes of the ancient world. These were special reserved seats located at the most ideal levels for the near perfect viewing of the spectacle below—high enough to see everything, low enough to feel part of the action. These were reserved for the powerful, wealthy, and VIPs of the Roman Empire.

The lesson for you as a marketer is to appeal to your most valuable clients in ways that make them feel special. Premium offerings that deliver tangible advantages to your clients are part of our cultural trading up phenomenon. Many people are willing to pay premium prices for premium offerings.

The Coliseum had two subfloors beneath its main stage to support the activities above. Elevators whisked animals, gladiators, participants, and props up at just the right time and dumped them out virtually anywhere. These Romans knew how to surprise.

Your marketing will be more effective when it is unexpected and a bit unpredictable. What breaks the expected and routine tends to stick in the minds of your prospects. And here is the secret, they like the surprise and appreciate your effort that goes into making one. Remember this: bore is a four-letter word!

The Roman Coliseum was built to last. It has weathered the day-to-day storms, frenzied crowds, and the unpredictability of Roman culture and its sometimes crazed emperors. It had forethought built in. Your marketing should be based on a system of forethought that uses known, effective methods. It should be able to weather the storms of economic change, adjust to the stream of life, and quickly resume its work even after changes in employ-ees, increases in postage costs and the ever-changing government rules of what you can and cannot do. If you are systemless, unpre-pared, or unadjustable, your marketing is in a precarious position. Successful systems exist that can do all this. Why use anything else?

The Roman Coliseum was a sight to behold in its day! Simply stated, it was grand. Its walls and columns and arches and portals were encased in marble. Beautiful. Huge flags flew from the top. It was designed to be pleasant in most any weather. Huge retractable awnings were deployed to protect the audience from the sun and rain. It was one of the architectural wonders of the day. It so ap-pealed to the human senses that it became the Roman version of what many call "the third place," not home and not work, but the place between where people gathered to just be.

As a marketer, when your brick-and-mortar location or website or representations of these are aesthetics in the architectural sense of the word—meaning a place one enjoys just being in—you have created your own version of a third place. It would be a mistake to discount this. When a patient enjoys your place or website, they stay longer, (linger, even) and buy more. One need only look at the current Las Vegas building boom and its recent luxury hotels to get confirming evidence.

The Coliseum in Rome, and all that came with it, provided an engineered experience. That shouldn't be surprising. The Romans were known for their engineering of roads, buildings, aqueducts, and monuments to victory. They had hot and cold running water! So it isn't a surprise that they conceived and executed an engi-neered experience.

They built each component to serve a different purpose that, when added up, left a wanted memory. The Coliseum and its pageantry, games, and happenings provided entertainment, education and an escape from daily living. News and events of the Empire were announced by heralds surrounding the Coliseum and within its walls.

Your practice should be engineered to leave a lasting positive memory too. The best marketing is to do what you do well and do it with a certain flourish that makes it fun and memorable. When you can mix in education, entertainment, and an escape from daily living, you have a winner that will be talked about on every conceivable communication channel by your clients.

The Coliseum and its games, events, and processions did another thing very well. It created emotions in the hearts of the attendees. On display was a new story everyday. Participants on the floor were cheered, booed, admired, and showered with attention. They were celebrities to the people of Rome. The fans in the stands were engaged and mentally stimulating themselves "playing" the games too. The grand stage of the Coliseum had winners, losers, life regained, and gruesome deaths. Often the "fans" were given the task of deciding a participant's fate. It was one huge continuing human interest story. Who would win? Who would lose? Who would die? Who would live? Unpredictable. Fascinating. A new surprise everyday.

The degree to which your marketing can engage the emotions of your clients and your prospective ones helps to determine how effective your marketing can be. Most marketing doesn't come close.

Great copy spins tales of human interest and persuasion that help the reader see himself in the story, to guide the reader to imagine himself owning the feelings that the offering brings.

It takes some doing. And it isn't just copy. You and your practice must vibrate with the values, needs, emotions, and desires of its clients and speak the language that resonates deep within them.

Who knew that the two-thousand-year-old Coliseum of Rome held such lessons?

The Three Sales You Must Make Before You Make the First One

Let's first understand that there are really four different sales. And the one everyone knows about is the last one—a patient says yes to your offering.

It's the first three 'sales' that help determine if you have a chance at all with the last one.

So, if the fourth sale is the one that creates the transfer of money to you, then what do one, two, and three do?

* The first sale you make, is to yourself.

It is your deep and abiding belief in the value you bring that allows you to make the three subsequent sales.

If you don't believe in your offering and its value, it is a virtual cinch that no one else will either. The sad truth is that too many dentists DO have high value results to offer to their customers, yet, for whatever reason, discount the true value. It is a lose-lose-lose situation.

Take a careful look at the value you bring, not only now, but also in the future for your client. You'll see much more than you have recognized before. (Often your patient needs to have that value illustrated for him.)

If you don't believe or can't believe in your offerings, find ones that you do believe in. This first sale sets up all subsequent ones.

* The second sale is to your team.

Your team must believe in what you do, the value of your offering, and what you charge for it. The more passionate they are about you and your offering, the easier it is to achieve the next two sales.

Here is the other side to this equation: if one or more of your team do not believe in you and your practice, your offering, its value, and the fee or price you charge, your third and fourth sales have a markedly less possibility for success. How much so? Try on 80 percent less (probably worse.) Call it the plague of not believing in you and what you do.

I call the belief in what you offer the invisible essence. It is the intangible, but ever so real and detectable sense one gets from communicating with the team. If they are believers, it is easier for your patients to be, too.

Just how important is this invisible essence? Some people use this invisible essence perception as the test whether they should buy or not. When you and your team "pass," they buy.

Oh, by the way, many of the skills of sales and persuasion are the same ones that leaders should be using with their "troops." Frankly, most leaders across the board fail to spend enough time and effort "selling" to their own teams about the company or practice and its offerings.

When your team are believers, you and your company or practice present a unified message. Before you discount this, think of any one business where a team or group member wavered or hesitated in recommending an offering to you. Did you buy? Did you say yes? NO is the self-evident and typical answer.

* The third sale is often overlooked—the sale of you.

This is the sale that the salesperson and company make to get the buy-in from the patient. The third sale is the sale of you and your practice as the best possible option. One that is liked and trusted. This is critical.

If your prospective patient likes you and trusts you, you are virtually halfway to the yes.

But hold on—you have probably known people you have liked but did not trust and vice-versa, right?

That's what the third sale is all about—creating likeability and creating trust. Likeability is tied to an interesting factor. I call this the I Like You Factor.

It is the principle of reciprocal liking. When someone indicates either overtly or indirectly that he likes you, your response is to reciprocate. Whether you state it or not, you mentally, usually unconsciously, say, "I like you too."

Seven sure-fire winners to set the stage for the I Like You factor:

* Be friendly. Take a genuine interest in the person.
* Find something you can like about her.
* Ask her questions about her life.
* Use good manners.

* Mirror her communication style—rate of speech, word choices and tone.
* Acknowledge and admire something that is important to her.
* Let her know by your words and actions that you like her.

Trust

Trust is another thing altogether. People have a kind of Trust Radar that tells them intuitively who to trust by all the clues and cues that the person gives off. For you, the most important item is to be a trustworthy person. People will get it.

Of course, your team is part of this equation, too. The "between us girls" conversation occurs all over the professional and business world. Your prospective patients (and even existing ones) will ask your team for their opinion about a suggested service or product you have suggested.

They see your team as not having the same level of self-interest as you do. To a prospect, your team members are the insiders who know the real poop.

Therefore, many will depend on this confidential conversation while you are not around as a primary trust test about the value of what you bring. So it had better be good. What can you do to ensure that it is? Forget trying to ban them. It would create suspicion in your prospect if her inquiry was rebuffed or given a token answer.

This conversation will occur. It won't be stopped. So, leverage it!

Talk about the "between us girls" concept to your team and then prepare them for what to say. Now your insiders can support you and your offerings. The big ah-ha is to prep the team for it. Here is the other ah-ha. Be who you say you are and deliver like you say you will. Then your team will gush out support for you.

If you aren't these things, your team will come off badly during these private, insider chitchats that so many prospects rely on as part of the way they buy.

There are many other ways to instill trust of you in another person by using proofs. These include testimonials of other patients, statistics of your successes, stories about successful work with patients, pictures of cases and projects completed, your expert status, your articles, and writings, as well your warranties and guarantees.

Being a respected expert eases the trust issues dramatically. All of these represent risk reduction for your patient—less risk in working with you increases the number of people who say yes to your highest and best offerings.

A further level of trust comes from being authentic. No one expects total perfection on every level, every time. What they do want to know about is the consistency of delivery and the likelihood of success while working with you. They want to know the potential risks and possible outcomes.

Most importantly, they want to feel they can trust you to do right by them. That is authentic. Omitting the potential problems in your discussions decreases trust and sets up expectations that you may not be able to fulfill.

Be open to tell of these potential problems up front, for this will defuse emotions that could go nuclear later. Just don't harp on these potential problems. Do use statistics of success. As an example, 98 percent of our clients come back to us—if it is true.

How can you consciously elevate the trust of those you serve? It can mean the difference between just getting by and stellar success.

White Florida Sand on a Black Beach of Hawaii

The sands of Hawaii and Florida are quite different. The sands of Hawaii are black because of the volcanic rock. If you take a cup full of white Florida sand and spread it over one of the black beaches of Hawaii, it disappears to the eye. No one would even notice. It is just too dispersed.

If you take that same cup of white sand and place it in a four-inch square of black beach, it is an unmistakable white sand beacon of marketing brilliance. It stands out. It gets noticed.

Your marketing should do the same to stand out.

Consider these two examples of white Florida sand on a black beach. With a media like television, you are better off having three ads in the same hour than three ads spread over the entire day. It is even better if those three ads are run at the same time, day after day. Repetition is built quickly in the audience that watches at those times.

In direct mail, you are better off mailing to a list of five thousand names three times over a relatively short period of time than fifteen thousand once with no follow-up. The results are markedly different.

You want your marketing to be like the cup of white sand on a small section of black sand beach. Concentrated. Impactful. Attention demanding.

What if you want a bigger part of the beach? Ah, we'll answer that in a minute. First, this warning: it takes some creativity to do this well. If you do stupid things to get noticed, that are so foreign to your offering that they seem inane or disconnected, you can reduce the reputation of your brand and reduce sales.

While stupid pet tricks get laughs, you had better be in the entertainment world or selling animal related offerings or have some connection you can make sensible to your audience.

Here are four principles of how to get noticed the right way so your marketing message gets through.

Principle 1: The Rule of Surprise

Anything that is unexpected gets your neurons to pay attention. In fact, purposely breaking an expected pattern is a sure winner in the attention-getting realm.

No matter the media, if it breaks conventional thinking, it will get noticed. It can't go too far though or it'll be discarded mentally as too confusing or too wacky to be real.

In our white sand on a black beach example, the contrast between the white and black is striking. It creates curiosity. Why is that white stuff here on this black beach? Your targeted public wants to know. It grabs them and pulls them in.

Try getting attention by placing white sand on a four inch square of white beach. Nothing. Nada. Zilch on the attention meter. It goes along with the expected. Ho-hum. The targeted public just keeps on going. And if it is a piece of direct mail, it will soon be nestled smartly with all the other pieces that failed the first rule to get attention—in the round file that the average person stands over while sorting the mail!

Now your message has to keep the attention so it flows into interest.

Principle 2: Demand for Salience

The junction of attention and interest demands a decision from the audience. The individual decides in about three seconds, from the first attention-getting moment to the backside of the initial interest moment, where he must answer, "How does this affect me? Why should I be interested?"

So there has to be at least a glimmer of gain or removal of pain perceptible to the individual, or all conscious attention dissolves. Your message is "discarded," and quick. Test this yourself while reading an ad or sales letter, listening to the radio, watching television. No gain or "solving my problem" or "removing my pain" and I am outta here.

If the transition moment from attention to interest is clumsy or difficult to grasp, again your message is "discarded."

It is at the interest moments that the salience and connection to your offering needs to be shaped. The stronger the salience (strength of message) to the individual, the deeper the interest builds. Most all of this is occurring in seconds. The process is largely unconscious, yet is always in operation.

Salience has many components. These include a problem needing solving or a previously desired want that is already part of the conversation going on in the mind of your client, to paraphrase

Robert Collier. If the offering is cultural or values aligned, there is more agreement potentially with the offering.

An easy example of a cultural value is the American cultural value of merit: those who work hard should be rewarded. For an American, that is an easy agreement. The entire country has had reward on merit as one of its founding values.

The stronger the salience of your message, the fewer times it must be repeated to induce action. If your house is on fire, it is darn salient for you to get the fire out, and now. Anything offered at the moment of the fire that'll help put it out is "on message" for you. You are buying and in a hurry.

So it is really about finding agreement for your offering with the problems, thoughts, values, and needs of the potential client. The more salient your offering, the more agreement there will be. The stronger the agreement, the more intensely a prospect will feel compelled to do what you ask.

In our white sand on a black beach example, attention is gained and then curiosity takes hold. Why is this white sand here on this black beach? Say, for example, the individual who notices it is a hotel developer; the white sand could represent a potential advantage for a new hotel if he could build one on a white sand beach in Hawaii where none existed before. It could solve his problem of creating a unique property that some travelers would like better than another hotel on a black sand beach. His hotel property would stand out.

Which brings us to the next principle…

Principle 3: Frequency of Repetition

If the white sand on the black beach was a message, the more cups of white sand concentrated in a small area of black beach there are, the more the message gets hammered home. One cup could get missed by someone further down the beach. He would never see it. But if it was repeated frequently enough in his sight, it would get his attention. This is what gets missed by the average unknowing dentist.

The tide would wash away the pile of the white sand on the black beach in a day's time, just as marketing messages get forgotten day to day as man falls into blissful sleep. The white sand on the black beach must be repeated enough that the memory of it sticks. Thus, it must be repeated and done frequently enough that it becomes remembered by long-term memory. The more salient a message is to an individual, the less it has to be repeated to be effective.

Principle 4: The Concept of Targeting

Targeting has everything to do with salience. It answers the question of who is the most likely prospect for this offering. Targeting is a way of selecting to whom a message will be sent. You are looking for the individual who has a problem, need, or goal that your offering solves, answers, or fixes. It really is the match game of marketing.

Matching your offering to its most likely prospect occurs in two ways. Both are designed to get the message to the probable prospective buyer. You can target by what you say and how you say it. This is done in broad reach media such as radio and television. Even here, some stations use demographics and viewership, listener data of its audience to sway potential advertisers to use their media as it "targets" their prospects.

When one's offering has mass appeal, mass media works when done well. In our white sand black beach example, it would be like announcing that a cup of white sand has been found on a small section of black beach.

Whether done as an ad or as a news announcement, those who deemed this important enough would wend their way to where it was. This is targeting based on what you say and how you say it to find prospective interested parties.

The problem now is that there are so many media channels, it is becoming increasingly harder to get enough eyeballs and ears paying enough attention to your messages so prospects self-select.

The solution is to buy more and more media, but that costs more and more money.

It is this reason that has forced direct mail into the position as one of marketing's big dogs.

Direct mail looks to target specific prospects based on location, age, gender, attitudes, interests, and past buying habits.

Mail lists can be selected on virtually any characteristic you can think of. Direct mail matches interests of prospective users and your offerings and then sends a message directly to them via the mail.

You should take note of the big digital companies including Google and Microsoft using direct mail to market their digital products as evidence of its efficacy.

How big is direct mail? Some say twice as much is spent on direct mail as all other media combined! The problem with direct mail generally is grabbing the attention of the reader long enough to get them interested and responding. There is so much mail vying for attention that it's harder every year to get direct mail read. The answer has been to target prospects by interest with increasing sophistication.

In our white sand on a black beach example, it would be like sending a postcard with a picture of the white sand on a small stretch of black beach to sand or beach aficionados or hotel developers or anyone interested in sand, and particularly white sand.

The postcard could also be used to grab attention and then create interest in anything to do with beaches, water sports, fishing, or any number of activities that could be reasonably connected to white sand on a black beach.

What about when you want to create a big effect along the entire length of a beach? Well, you would have to bring enough sand that it did not get dispersed away. This could require several dump truck loads and even then it would require one to concentrate the sand together in big clumps, safe from the tides and in plain view of everyone on the beach.

If you need to create a big effect marketing-wise with a large group of potential clients, you had better be ready to spend lots of time, money, and effort to make sure enough prospects notice what you have. It will take repetition, the right frequency, and salience to get through.

Sometimes the smallest lessons yield the biggest results.

Getting attention is the first small thing your marketing should accomplish. A question you could ask yourself about your marketing's attention quotient: is it like a cup of white sand on a small tract of black sand beach?

Too Many

There is such a thing as too many or too much when marketing your practice (or any business). Much marketing is wasteful. How much? From a low of 50 percent to as high as 90 percent!

How can this be? By being TOO.

You may have heard: those who try to be everything to everybody end up being nothing for everyone—or some version that is similar. And it is true.

Just as limiting what you provide in services has the effect in elevating you as a "specialist."

So too does limiting what you are saying with your marketing messages. It elevates your message into being registered within your reader or listener so to speak.

Too many different messages within any single marketing piece in any media dilute the message and inhibit the core message from being heard.

You do have a core message, don't you? A single core message is what is most effective. Say too many things and you leave your reader or listener confused. The confused person's first action is to stop, to not act, delay, to think about it (if they have gotten that far). Most people just mentally dump any confusing message or anything they don't understand. So be clear. Be understandable. Fast.

Too Many Media

This is the error that just costs you. Only large budget (millions usually) marketers can afford to be everywhere. You cannot unless you just enjoy watching your dough being wasted.

Pick a media and then work that one media until it is full—I mean really full. THIS is what gets you recognized and makes your name known.

People talk with each other. You don't have to be everywhere to market effectively. Become known in that one media first.

Too Many People Trying to Be Reached

Few can afford to "talk" to huge masses all at once. You are far better off speaking to fewer people more often than talking to alot one or two times. Frequency of your message is more critical than reach of your message.

This is a big one and often missed by even savvy marketers. Focus your message, limit your media, and repeat your message frequently to a smaller group that makes sense for your budget.

How You Sell

Sold Because He Had To

Bahamas Island

His name was Perry. Perry McPhee. He was our tour guide to Nassau this morning. We had not planned on taking a tour. Then we met Perry. He was standing just off the pier. He walked up and asked how much time we had on the island. We told him 3 and 1/2 hours. He launched into his affable spiel, easing our tensions. The whole tour for all five of us would be $25 a person.

I liked him. He then offered something that I have never heard from a tour guide—a guarantee! "Sir, if you don't like the tour, you pay me nothing in the end."

I huddled with my family. It was time for family lessons. The kids giggled, my wife, Holly, nodded approvingly.

"Now Perry, how about 20 dollars a person?"

Perry remained unfazed, smiled, and came right back at me. "Sir, how about this, I accept your offer of 100 dollars for the tour and if I do as good of a job for you as I say I will, you give me the extra $25?!"

I liked this guy's moxie. He had style and confidence.

"You've got yourself a deal," I replied while I shook his hand. Perry had done several things right. The very first was that he sold himself and did it in the first 30 seconds.

Think about how you "evaluate" others. Most people "size peo-ple up" quickly based on appearance, communication, facial cues, mannerisms, and attitude. Remarkably, these first impressions are usually accurate in as little as seven seconds.

Perry was "on stage" in these critical first seconds. He knew it. He had trained himself to engage his potential tour client, create trust, and set up the conversation for a yes. Almost half of any sales decision is made based on trust and likeability.

How do you come across to first-time patients?! Do you need to consider the lesson from Perry? Become good at persuasion because the quality of your life depends on it.

Whaling

Every casino wants them

They get all sorts of freebies, benefits, and inducements—free air travel, suites, food, drinks. If they are big enough, they can ask for and get just about anything they want.

These people are known as whales. Literally meaning they will bet a LOT of money and likely lose a big bag of dough, too. It pays the casinos to cater to this type of guest. In fact, it pays them so well that specific hostesses are assigned to act as concierges to them.

The average guest receives none of this. His value as a guest is so far less that the casino cannot afford to do much, if anything, for this "Little Guy."

Are you surprised that the casinos figured this out long ago?

They know what helps them build those over the top, palatial hotels and resorts with enormous gaming areas. The largest of these in the world is, of course, Las Vegas. It is viewed as an entertainment mecca and a fitting place for celebrations, bachelor and bachelorette parties, and quickie weddings. Experientially, it is composed of entertainment, escapism, aesthetics, and no small amount of education.

They are the best whalers in the world. They know that size matters! How many whales are there at the typical casino? Not that many. They are only a small percentage of the total visitors.

Casinos are smart. They do everything they can to glorify the experience of being a whale so other non-whales want to move up. The casinos have created a pecking order. Within the culture of gambling, a whale has more status and importance.

And, since virtually everyone has an eternal need to feel important, the casinos feed the need and smile all the way to the bank.

Bam. Here are three quick lessons from people who know how to make a lot of money.

* Segment your list of clients so you know what kind of client is the most profitable.
* Treat your best clients differently than everyone else.
* Make becoming a best client desirable.

The Make Me Feel Important Rule

Why this rule continues to get overlooked amazes me. What people will do to get recognition boggles the mind. Reality shows are filled with people who are willing to sacrifice all sorts of personal information and appear the fool for fifteen minutes of fame.

The wealthy contribute billions to have their names attached to their philanthropy. Now the practice of philanthropy has become part of the responsibilities of the rich.

The reality is that we are all built the same. It is human nature to want to feel important.

Smart dentists feed the need. By doing so you can ease your work, enhance your relationships, and grow your business or practice at a pace that will make you the envy of your competitors and colleagues.

Your most affluent, successful, and well-to-do clients and prospective clients have a larger need for recognition than normal. Why? The answer lies in what they have accomplished and their position.

Few are the successful who have anyone that openly gives them the admiration they deserve. Yes, I said deserve. If you look at what they have accomplished, you would agree that they have gone past "average man." Often their colleagues are envious of them. Their enemies damn them.

Their families treat them as if they were just like everybody else (because to them they are). If you show me any high-achieving individual, very few of them have ever received the kudos they want.

The make me feel important rule as been around for as long as man. It has been written about for centuries. Yet, comparatively, it is the most ignored of all human needs.

It is the tool used by colleges to get their alumni to part with a sizable portion of their accumulated net worth. "Yes, we will be glad to re-name our school in your name." Evidence: Duke University was re-named early in the twentieth century after a wealthy donor gave them a fortune.

The Michigan School of Business was renamed the Ross School of Business upon the donation of 100 million from an alumnus.

If you can become a bit inventive, you'll find dozen of ways to keep this ever-endearing principle capturing patients for you. And it never gets old. Done well, the patient never wants to leave you.

Understand and Apply the Power of Transaction Size

How much more money, time, and effort does it take to service your best patients? Answer: more than it costs to handle the average patient. But how much more is it? Hmmmmmm. Your profits come from the difference between your costs to deliver your services, experiences, and transformations, and what you get paid to do so.

OK, no great news there. And there are three points that do need hammering home.

* The difference between a big fee client and a little fee client, in terms of delivering what you do, stacks up favorably for the big fee/price client.

The overhead costs just aren't that much more to serve the big client. Yes, it will take more of your time, energy, efforts, and smarts, but overall, the leverage of your efforts occurs with the client who spends the most with you.

The added bonus is that often the big client is easier to work with, more appreciative, and allows you to perform your highest and best services. All of this yields professional and personal satisfaction.

* How many clients do you need to hit your productivity targets per year?

Let's do the numbers. Let's assume you want a million dollars of gross income. How many clients do you need to hit your target?

* If each client is worth 200 dollars, you need 5,000 clients.
* If each client is worth 1,000 dollars, you need 1,000 clients.
* If each client is worth 2,000 dollars, you need 500 clients.
* If each client is worth 10,000 dollars, you need 100 clients.
* If each client is worth 50,000 dollars, you need 20 clients.
* If each client is worth 100,000 dollars, you need 10 clients.
* If each client is worth 250,000 dollars, you need 4 clients.
* If each client is worth 500,000 dollars, you need 2 clients.
* If each client is worth 1,000,000 dollars, you need 1 client.
* The fewer the clients you need, the faster you hit your goal.

Not every client has the potential of high value. Many have no need for your highest and best service. Unfortunately, too many times professionals fail to bring those who do need that to the point of saying yes.

The type, scope, and breadth of your marketing and costs of that marketing are vastly different depending on the average unit purchase or case size.

* The third point has to do with decreasing costs. As you serve fewer clients, you need fewer people and smaller offices. The costs of your organization decreases overall. Smaller groups are easier to manage. So the spread increases between your costs of delivery and your fee/ price…and so do your profits.

The challenge is to continually create and coordinate a professional practice that effectively serves fewer patients, delivering your highest and best services, experiences, and transformations at larger fees. For many, the problems of doing so are overwhelming. Many want to do this, but lack proven methods to get there.

You Can Do What Casinos Can't

The gaming industry has a problem with whales. It is finding enough of them.

The gaming whale knows he is in demand. It is a certain persona that has the financial wherewithal, temperament, and schedules to visit that little-bit naughty fantasyland known as Las Vegas. There aren't that many, so public relations, marketing, and sales efforts circle the world. They are selling an experience as a gain. That is a tougher sale than you have to make.

Most of your patients think first about fixing problems, then the possibility of gain.

Gaming really doesn't fix any problems, although it can create quite a few. You do fix problems through your services, experiences, and transformations.

But there is more to it. When you are at your best, you can find plenty of whales, because you can make them.

How is that?

While many patients have an idea of their problems, usually it is a gross underestimation. It is human nature to tend to gloss over these. You can diagnose problems and opportunities previously unknown or unrealized.

No matter what your field is, you can engage your patient in an audit or diagnostic session designed to root out the problems they face. Most patients and prospects have an utter lack of fully understanding the depth of problems they have and future implications if left untreated or unsolved.

In other words, you help them find problems they did not know they had and then make the effects of them real to your client. Voilà, you have made a whale.

The beauty of this is that you have served your patient well for doing so. You have used your superior knowledge, training, skills, talents, and abilities to find problems and present solutions that improve the quality of life of your patient. You have become the trusted guide they have often sought, but have failed to find.

Features to Benefits Stops Short of the Sales Finish Line?

Fatal Omission?

It is one of those "everyone knows" kind of things. You know, sell the sizzle, not the steak. Only it isn't enough.

Crap. All this time just about everybody has been telling you to sell the benefits of your offering. Only it isn't enough if you want to carry through to making the sale.

Yet, here is the answer to why likeability and relationship are some of the keys to sales. Now, likeability and relationships are not new ideas at all, either. Let's get concrete here. Imagine your spouse decides it is time to have a new house. The kids have grown up and moved out. You are thinking to downsize. She isn't. In fact, the house comes with more space and more of just about everything else. She wants fancy-schmancy—granite countertops, multiple fireplaces, outdoor kitchen, and a shower big enough for a gaggle of people. It has a card room and pantry big enough to lay in stores until the next millennium. It is a real beaut. Yep, she is shooting for the Designer House—the one that wins awards in the parade of homes or the charity benefit event.

Suddenly you are feeling like the house you are in right now is just fine. She is having no part of it. It is a new time—time for the house she did not know she had to have until her friend, Jamie, showed her new one off to the garden club. Her eyes became aware of the possibilities and there went your stash of cash!

What happened? Your dear ol' spouse got a bad case of home inadequacy. She now feels a gap between what was once OK and what is now required to feel complete in her domestic surroundings.

She is suffering from Gap-osis Disease. Boy, is that ever a powerful motivator! Hire the moving truck—you have a new address coming soon. The reality is that you should be consciously work-ing to create the Gap-osis Disease in everyone you can for your offering.

Cold Stone Creamery is a premium ice cream store that does a lot of things right, marketing-wise. They have even named the sizes of their ice cream at a feelings level. One of the choices is "Gotta Have It," a big, heaping portion of tantalizing treat with your name on it.

It is your ability to connect the dots of understanding between the features to benefits to feelings that determine your success in persuasion at all levels.

You should be selling the feelings that come with your offer-ing. Yep, it is the feelings that you are selling. Speak to benefits and lead to the feelings she'll have. It is the feelings that you are beckoning, the ones you arouse that make the difference between yes and no.

The more you leave the arousal to her, the more unpredictable success becomes. Your job is to become Arousal Man or Arousal Gal to ensure that nothing gets lost in translation, that the dots get connected. It isn't easy, but the more you know, the better you can become.

There are two levels of feelings: the ones you can help your client have as a result of possessing the offering (the experience of "using" it) or the ones your client gets to enjoy while receiving it—the offering is the experience and its subsequent memory. If you can engage both, you really score.

The easiest thing would be to directly indicate the feelings to be had. And that method is fraught with danger of going past what is acceptable to say. You had best be invited or know that you can go to this land of personal intimacy.

You have four choices. The simplest of the four is to let the patient connect the dots herself. The problem is that the client may never put two and two together for herself.

The next choice is to hint at it, around it, hoping she'll get the hint. This is better than letting her be self-connecting, but still unreliable.

The next choice is to tell her directly. The problem is that you had better know her well enough that you understand what is important to her and that she trusts you enough to let you "in" to the inner feelings sanctum. Thus, the likeability and relationship factors mean she is more likely to let you go there.

The fourth choice is to let others tell the story for you. Use your team or, better, your patients, past and present, to provide the social proof by testimonials. Good testimonials are almost always underused. They are the success stories that engage the hearts and minds of your patients at a feelings level. What better proof than the successes of credible people and the good feelings they have about you and your offering?

Likeability and Relationship

The better she feels about you, the easier it is for her to say yes. This is a feelings transference that is not particularly logical. What people do is to equate the feelings for you as feelings for your offering—and her experience has told her it works out to be true most of the time—logic or not.

Fear

Feelings of fear become larger with higher prices and fees. The higher the price or fee for your offering, the more complex the feelings that are involved, how many, and how they are related. If fear of having services performed or delivered is also present, you have a double whammy to overcome.

Fear is like a giant defective lens that warps your client's views of the choices you offer. You must get your client to "see straight" or you'll get a big fat no, either quietly or by the patient wanting to think about it or by a loud, crashing vocal, Hell to the No, given with authority. You must quiet these fears to have any hope of making the sale.

The best marketing helps relieve these fears before your prospective client ever sees you. The best case presentation processes likewise answer these fears in advance. Does yours?

The Power Beyond Emotion

The first point to realize is that people say they buy for logical reasons. Nope. The reality is they use logic as an alibi to buy, especially when it comes to products and services that are expensive.

An affluent consumer buys a new Lexus for 88K. His reason he says he buys the Lexus: it had good resale value or it's rated high by Consumer Reports or it is safer or, or, or. The alibi he uses with himself and with others who ask him why he bought an eighty-eight-thousand dollar car. It is logic. Oh boy, the trap of thinking that is why people buy.

The sad reality is that most dentists have tried to use education and logic to get large ticket items or services purchased, only to have their heads handed to 'em. But, they have heard so many times from teachers and sales gurus that education is all that is needed. Nope again.

Back to our consumer, he could have bought a twelve-thousand-dollar car. It would have served to get him from place to place.

Our affluent consumer wouldn't dream of it. No, the affluent consumer buys the Lexus because it represents something more than logic and even more than emotion. It is an identification emblem.

As you know, it is physiologically impossible for a person to make a decision without emotion. But, there is a deeper truth that is more fundamental than the reality of emotional decision-making.

There is a deeper emotional level that goes to our brain stem, the limbic system also known as our reptilian brain. It is this part of our brain that develops earliest. Here is where the values and emotions are most deeply seated. It is as close to instinct as man has. This is the place where the values, mores, and beliefs of a culture exist. It varies from one culture to another.

Welcome to the world of ethnography. This is the study of cultural mores and beliefs. The U.S. is different from Canada and France and England and every other country on the planet.

Major international corporations now have these cultural anthropologists on their teams. The game has changed again.

The reality is that everything has become more sophisticated. What once worked no longer does.

Again, back to our affluent consumer. Why did he buy the eighty-eight-thousand dollar Lexus? I can't say for sure. A further truth: seldom does an affluent consumer or any consumer know the deep-seated, instinctive, cultural, emotional "reason" he buys that vehicle.

Our culture has never had an aristocracy. We had no king to kill or overthrow. We have never had a way to be knighted or receive titles. Our culture is one that is based on merit. We have a meritocracy.

We are the land of new money. In fact, we as a culture think less of those who were born into money. We honor and celebrate our entrepreneurs. Only in America could a young geeky kid develop an operating system for computers and become one of the richest men in the world. Our most successful business leaders and entertainers become cultural icons and celebrities. We even elect these celebrities to high office. Think Ronald Reagan and Arnold Schwarzenegger and Donald Trump.

For Americans, money represents proof of success, goodness, and a high level of survival. The car represents an outward badge; it represents having "made it." It is about bragging rights, even if the owner never overtly says a word. What does this mean for you? Always look beyond the logic a client gives you to the emotions and unspoken, deeper- seated cultural beliefs if you want to move a client to say yes. What could you do to understand these motives better?

Is She Buying or Are You Selling?

It makes a difference...a huge difference.

When you sell, the first reaction is what? Unless you are unusual in how you are wired, you'll see that you first respond by putting up your defenses; a mini-wall goes up the moment you or virtually anyone else senses that she/he is being sold something. It is the normal response. One of the reasons that people like going on the Internet or using Consumer Reports type magazines is that they feel they are getting unbiased information.

This is a way of coping with the need to buy without having to deal with pushy, confrontational sales people.

People normally like to acquire things—they like to buy based on the choices they make. People like to buy, but hate being sold.

Alas, this creates a problem for anyone in the influence and persuasion game. The process must be planned to avoid confrontation so common in push selling. Push selling is what the average Homo sapiens considers selling to be.

Frankly, it is an ugly sight—visions of hucksters in loud sport coats talking fast, while slipping their hands into our pockets to fish out our wallets come to mind.

Push selling by its nature invites resistance. It can evoke the old "you push me, I'll push you back" scenario.

Typically, the push sale becomes a battle of wits, with a winner and loser. No one wants to lose in the process. As our populace has become more sophisticated and aware of the tricks of the push sale techniques, they have also decided that anyone pushing to sell something is inherently wrong.

It isn't by accident that the terms pushy salesman and pusher have become pejorative terms.

If you ever become involved in a "battle" to get anyone to do something, with constant objection handling and the like, realize that you are using push sale techniques.

Even if you are good at push selling, it is not a good long-term relationship builder. Push selling has long since lost its usefulness, particularly for complex situations like ours.

The Winning Way has been called magnetic sales or attraction sales or pull persuasion. While it has the components of consultative selling, it is really bigger than that by a lot. The Winning Way is persuasion that has the prospective buyer pulling himself to your offering because it matches with who he is and what he wants.

It has hundreds of component pieces, which must fit together precisely as the gears on a Swiss handmade watch. While few fully understand the Winning Way with all its components, even those who do often don't bother.

The good news is that you can learn this, for I have laid out the steps so you can get there. The process of persuasion with the Winning Way must be precisely choreographed with planning for any contingency.

The designed persuasion experience must subtly attract. It is akin to a romantic seduction that has the players on both sides of the relationship delighting in the process. OK, it might not be that much fun, but it is an enjoyable experience for all parties.

The Winning Way has the integrity of only persuading those who have a genuine need or want that you can fulfill. Pull persuasion is part of a total system that seamlessly integrates marketing and sales into one continuous channel, gently guiding to the inevitable magical yes.

It is a philosophy that leaves all parties winning. It requires a willingness to do whatever it takes to become an ethical influencer.

The Winning Way has three components that are most often missed in traditional persuasion training: your certainty, your confidence, and your control.

* How certain are you about yourself and your services?
* How confident are you in what you do?
* How much control are you willing to exert over yourself, your team, and your patients to get the result?

Your answers, given honestly, will be revealing. Do you dare answer them? If you are really interested in improving your case presentation, ask your team to answer those three questions anonymously about you.

The Emotional Aftertaste of the Sale

You have probably tasted it. It is nearly that palatable. Sometimes you savor it. It is sweet. It leaves an emotional aftertaste to be relished like a fine Cabernet. This is the sale gone right.

Sometimes the emotional aftertaste is entirely different. Sometimes it feels like you have thrown up in your mouth from the sales experience.

What makes the difference?

It is how the seller approaches the entire process of selling. At once, powerfully, you know the answer to the question: why do people hate to be sold? When you can answer that question exactly, you have the key to the secret formula for off the charts persuasion success.

What if I gave you the answer right now? What would that be worth to you? I know. I know. A LOT.

Let's take a look at a typical situation with a buyer and a seller. A seller is ready and eager to get you to say yes.

A buyer is "not all that interested" at first, until something "catches his eye." The seller launches into his sales spiel. He is selling by a process that he has developed or been taught, or just by the seat of his pants. The buyer, meanwhile, launches into how he buys. He has a way to buy, usually unconscious even to him.

How often do you feel these match naturally? Can you hear the sound of sales friction like fingernails on a chalkboard when they don't? Can you see the unwelcome picture of it all in your mind, recalling all the times you had to suffer through the sales clod's unprofessional attempts to sell you?

It isn't pretty. Oh, sure, the social graces kick in and prevent meltdowns and outright violence, but how much better could it be? How much better should it be?

Buyers want to buy; yet, they have their own experiences and the experiences of others that have taught them to be on guard against being taken advantage of or paying too much or making the wrong choice.

Yet, the buyer wants to able to trust the sales person. It is a real chore to be on guard all the time. This is the reason that the second sale is easier to make after you as a seller have successfully delivered what you promised. The buyer has come to trust you more. The entire sales process goes more smoothly and more comfortably for both parties.

Buyers want trusted sales guides who have their interest at heart. Buyers start out with questions, statements, and indications of interest with their body language. These sales hints are often masked, disguised, or hidden. The buyer is checking out the seller on two counts: his offering and who he is.

Many sellers are so busy giving their spiel that they miss these vital sales hints—to their loss. These sales hints hold the secrets to creating a satisfying sales experience for all parties.

But like so many things, the failure to communicate occurs when the seller doesn't match the way the buyer buys. Sales fizzle instead of sales sizzle.

The buyer gets uncomfortable. It shows. In some cases, the seller, sensing that the sale is going the wrong way, increases the speed and volume of his language. The buyer is doing the internal squirm. It is as if the seller thinks that if he can just get the client to listen to his words, then the client won't be able to listen to the little voices in his head getting progressively louder, finally going off in booming salvos of negativity, screaming to get out of there.

The longer the seller keeps applying sales pressure, the worse it gets. The seller often increases the force of words as if the sales pressure can force the buyer into a sales capitulation. This can occur where the buyer relents and buys just to get rid of the seller.

Two things will occur when this happens. First, that is the end of any possible future sales. Second, the emotional aftertaste of the sale will ferment into a powerful sales poison that kills the reputation of the seller in the minds of all that hear of this special brand of buyer's remorse. And you can be assured that word of mouth has never been as powerful as today with the Internet just a few clicks away.

When more is at stake in a sales decision, then just buying to get rid of the seller seldom occurs. The buyer just moves away from the seller as quickly as possible, reminding all that will listen that this seller is a pox upon the buying world.

Sales events seldom get this abusive or aberrative. I deliberately showed just how wrong sales can go when sellers ignore the buyer's communication and insist on selling their way.

Ugly. Ugly. Ugly.

No buyer on earth likes these scenarios. Nor does any sane seller. Hmmmmm. Now if it just so happens that the buyer needs what the seller is selling, it is a lose-lose situation.

There is a better way.

First Lesson: The Buyer Has A Way Of Buying

It is the seller's responsibility to find out what it is. Information like that is hidden, but can be found by the gracious art of asking questions that yield answers.

Guess what? Virtually every buyer wants to have the seller find his way of buying. The buyer wants to be sold on his terms. That way he feels like he is buying, not being sold. People love to buy—and hate being sold.

The feeling of being sold occurs whenever the seller sticks to his way of selling when it ignores the buyer way of buying.

The real pro in persuasion works with the buyer to understand what is wanted and needed and then works as a committed guide to helping the buyer overcome his internal squirm AND like the persuasion process to boot.

The Dance of Romance can be a near perfect example of persuasion gone right. Boy meets girl. Girl likes boy. Boy likes girl. They then set out to communicate with one another at increasingly deeper levels, testing the waters so to speak. They both want it to work. It is a process.

Like romance, selling high valued offerings takes time to communicate the value of the offering. The amount of time needed to sell varies depending on the individuals involved, how big the problems are, and the value of your solution.

In romance, there is the first date where the couple gets to know each other. Offers of marriage do not occur successfully at this time.

In selling significant solutions to big problems, the first meeting is generally not a good time to sell your big solution. The trust and liking levels just aren't there yet. It has to develop, warm up.

Second Lesson: The Seller Needs A Way Of Selling

Yep, that's right. The seller needs a system of selling, one that he can reliably use to sell successfully.

Consider this system to be the road map to the client's Yes City. The reality that follows is that as soon as you reach the outskirts of Yes City, you must "call" the client to get directions to where his yes lives exactly. This requires asking questions and "directions" to what is most needed, wanted, and desired.

This is the art and science of asking progressively intrusive questions that yield up the information the seller can use to get the yes so everyone wins. A common mistake is rigidity of the system. Your sales system should be like putty. It has substance and it can adapt itself solidly to any situation as the client reveals the unique characteristics of his problems.

Imagine this sales putty fitting into all the spaces, holes, nooks, and crannies that your client wants you to fill to solve his problems.

Another common mistake is having the wrong person(s) making the sale.

Just as there are talents for numbers, systems, athletics, science, you name it, so too is there talent for selling. Your best salespeople get a "personal charge" out of creating the sale. If you don't come by the sales talent naturally, don't fret. Sales can be taught. What may be more important than talent for persuasion is the belief and passion for the offering being sold.

Fervent belief goes a long way in transferring a feeling of faith in the offering from the seller to the buyer. It is a reassurance for the buyer that the seller speaks with such conviction.

Third Lesson: Make A Sale To Get A Client And Create A Relationship... Then Work To Keep It

Did your buyer buy your offering once, never to do it again? If yes, your sales future is dim. Did you make a sale, gain a client and a relationship? If yes, congratulations. You have come down on the right side of the sales equation. The purpose of virtually all first sales is to gain a client.

To get this first sale, it can take a lot of hard work. The value isn't in that first sale, but in the future sales that are virtually guaranteed after acquiring a client who looks to you for help and guidance.

When you do the math, the second and third and all subsequent sales are the ones that bring the profit. There is no more cost of acquisition.

But there are two forgotten costs. First is the cost of serving the client after the sale has been made. These are very real costs and must be planned on as part of your original price for your offering or built into the offering as a continuity cost that the client expects to pay.

The second cost is the cost to continue to market to your existing clients, to defend your clients from those competitors who poach, who steal covertly or overtly. Large corporations do this all the time to defend their position in the market with individual buyers.

Coca-Cola continues to spend about five percent of its budget to defend the brand and keeps its users feeling good for choosing Coca-Cola.

Small businesses and professionals forget they have to do the same! When you compare your costs of acquiring a new client versus what you must spend to keep them a client, continually buying from you and aware of what you offer, the scales tip to the "keep 'em" side with resounding thud.

It is not uncommon for a practice or business to spend three hundred dollars to a thousand dollars or more to acquire a client/customer/patient or patron and then go cheap, refusing to spend five percent of that cost to keep them.

When you don't charge enough for what you provide, you can easily go stupid cheap—refusing to spend a paltry sum to keep a client and continue to sell them more. At least make the smart decision to spend "keep 'em" money on your good clients.

The Fourth And Last Lesson: The Psychological Contract Of A Sale

This one may surprise you. Every sale has within it an implicit promise of performance, trustworthiness, and truthfulness in doing business with you. This goes unrecognized by too many.

For the seller, once the sale has been made, the tension associated with the sale goes down. He can relax and enjoy his success in making the sale.

For the buyer, once the sale is made, the tension goes up! The buyer is wondering if he made the right decision. Will the seller come through as promised? Have I been a smart consumer? Did I make a wise decision?

These are all natural questions that every buyer faces as those little voices inside his head resonate with these and possibly many more questions.

So what is your responsibility as the seller?

In sales, silence is not golden. It is death to a sale. Even after the ink has dried on the sales agreement, this sales dissonance disease must be recognized and treated before it festers and infects the mind of your new client with doubts and misgivings.

Here is what to do to inoculate against this scourge, sales dissonance disease.

Seven Keys to Eliminating Sales Dissonance Disease

Makes 'em feel good for having bought. Congratulate him on the wisdom of his decision. Reassure him that you will deliver as promised. If possible, send a personal note or card of congratulations via the mail right away.

Tell them it is not unusual to have second thoughts and doubts. This is all normal and to be expected. Do suggest that he refrain from discussing the decision with family and friends who are un-informed about this problem and his decision to act as they are ill-prepared to advise him without all the information.

Again, shape and define the buyer's expectancies on your terms. You should have shaped these expectancies during the process of the sale anyway. When a purchase decision is made, the buyer has his own expectancies about what should happen next—failing to supply the buyer with what he should expect allows him to set his own rules and expectancies—and you are hopelessly behind.

The problem with that scenario is that you may not be able to deliver. Make a promise you can deliver. Tell them what will happen next and what they must do to participate actively in helping the promise of your offering actually be delivered.

Nail down your financial agreement and get a payment of your fee. That is a very real show of commitment. Preferably, a payment in full with associated discounts. If you can get that done, it will put all the financial decisions to bed forever. If not possible, get a definitive agreement and dates when payments will be made.

Continue to communicate with the buyer, answering questions and concerns as they come up. Follow-up is part of your implicit promise. Your buyer will have an increased desire for communication with you as the seller after the sale is made.

Start delivery of your offering right away or as quickly as possible. Once the decision to buy is made and agreed, your buyer wants your offering as speedily as you can deliver.

Closing Thoughts

Sales is about agreement, not force. Force creates resistance—the opposite of what a seller wants. Every buyer is looking to solve a problem. Whether the problem is causing present difficulties or is a want that is desired, the result for the professional seller is the same: help the buyer fix it.

The only way to create agreement is to decipher the values and thoughts of the buyer and then shape these artfully into new information and persuasion that matches the heart and mind of the prospect.

A sale gone right leaves the buyer with the sweet emotional aftertaste that every professional seller wants to leave behind.

What emotional aftertaste are you leaving behind?

How You Work

"Saddle Up Boys"

The 80/20 Rule Rides Again

Every time you think that you have gotten away from it, the guiding "rule" first developed by the Italian economist Pareto in studying the distribution of ownership land in Italy in 1906. He found that 80 percent of the land was owned by just 20 percent of the families.

Since that time, a slew of other observations have been based on some variant of this rule first found by observation.

* The rule is really an observation of human nature. That is why it continues to repeat itself.

Here is another reality. If you could somehow magically divide up all the income of a population equally among everyone, within a short period of time, the wealth would once again find its way back to the 80/20 rule.

The 80/20 rule can be found in just about every human endeavor and experience. Here are some examples. See if they fit for you.

* When 80 percent of your customers give you 20 percent of your income.
* When 80 percent of your problem clients come from 20 percent of your client/patient base.
* When 20 percent of your team get 80 percent of the meaningful work done.
* When 20 percent of your efforts yield 80 percent of your results.

The breakdown could be 70/30 or 90/10; the point is that there will be some variant of this rule of humankind within your business or practice and everywhere else too.

The 20-20 Rule

There is an even more enlightening concept I call the 20-20 rule. This is concerned with the 20 percent of your client base that is your most productive. Here is the kicker: 20 percent of your most productive 20 percent will yield 80 percent of income from that group of your clients.

This means that a mere four percent of your clients can give you 64 percent of your income. (I have seen it higher.) So the 80/20 rule lives inside the 20 percent too!

Go and compare your own practice or business's income by this rule of thumb. I am betting you'll find something similar to 20 percent of your clients yield 80 percent of your income. And the breakdown will further bring the truth of the 20-20 rule.

Ten Principles and Concepts of Working with Your 80/20 and Your 20/20

* Segment Your Client Base

Wouldn't it make sense that if 80 percent of your income is coming from this 20 percent, you should figure out a way to spend extra time with these clients?

Then, of course, there is the top 20 of the top 20, as well. Shouldn't you give even more time and attention to these elite of your best clients? That is just four percent of your entire client base! You can afford to pamper them a little, communicate with them more often. A better statement is that you can't afford not to!

Segmenting your client base by productivity and net income from each is smart business. Your biggest users know they are profitable for you. They have it figured out and, generally, they don't mind. In fact, they LIKE IT. They feel they deserve it. (And they do!)

What they do mind is you and your team failing to give the attention, communication, and amenities they feel they deserve.

Smart professional and business owners play this up with the nodding approval of their best customers. You can afford to spend extra time and effort with your best clients.

* **Twenty Percent are Willing to Pay More**

Here is a pearl: if all your clients pay you about the same fees or prices, there are around 20 percent of them who will pay you more for a different or higher level of service. That is a big one you can take to the bank.

* **The Rule Also Applies to the Time of Day!**

For many, 80 percent of their results occur in just 20 percent of their hours. Finding and preserving your most productive times for productive work is something everyone can do, starting immediately.

* **The Best Referrals**

An added bonus of selectively catering to your most profitable clients is the referrals they produce. Typically, your best clients will refer other prospective clients of similar qualities to themselves so they are also likely to be a top 20 type of client. It is the birds of a feather flock together rule.

* **Warning: Your Biggest Fee Patient May NOT Be Your Most Profitable**

This is a caveat that should be your concern. Just because a client pays you a big fee or buys a lot from you DOES NOT MEAN IT IS

A PROFITABLE TRANSACTION or patient. Far from it. The real profit comes from the difference between your cost of delivery of your offerings and what you charge for them. A big, demanding situation has hidden costs of delivery that are missing in smaller, less challenging cases.

Costs of delivering complex offerings can easily be geometric multiples of the smaller, simpler ones. Complex services should be charged out commensurate with what you must do, difficulty of accomplishment, degree of care, skill, judgment, and knowledge required. You can also consider how much hand holding and emotional costs that will be involved.

Invariably, in large or complex offerings you will be forced to spend significant time with logistics, arranging and rearranging schedules, phone time, chasing up all the little bits and pieces that make up the delivery of your services, experiences, and transformations. Finally, you could consider your unique ability to get results for your patient over all other alternatives.

(Warning: you have to clearly point this out and have your patient agree that it is true or face rejection and a downhill slide to economic ruin.)

* **Strategic Planning**

What would change about your strategy and other planning if you included this thinking at a strategic level? What could you do differently?

How could you leverage your time by using this thinking?

* What are the 20 percent of things you do so well that you can't be replaced?
* What are the 80 percent that can?

* What would happen if you delegated the 80 percent?
* What would happen if you concentrated only on the 20 percent of the 20 percent of what you do that brings you 64 percent of your income?
* Where are you wasting your time doing things that others can do for you?
* Keep 80/20 and 20/20 Thinking in the Forefront of Your Thinking Daily

It is the instant reminder of the priorities you have to keep in mind. It is the instant test to measure what you should concentrate on. It keeps you focused.

Bits and Pieces

Like all rules of thumb, it is sometimes another finger that counts, not just the thumb; you cannot just think with this and apply it indiscriminately—it takes some judgment.

Every group of ideas will break down into the 20 percent that are the most valuable and 20 percent of those that will be most-most valuable. The challenge is to find the most and most-most valuable ones out of the group.

You can't flush away the 80 percent because it is the platform from which the 20 percent emerges. It gives you depth and diversity. It gives you presence and stability. Often, clients can ascend into the top 20. On the other hand, you can lose a top 20 by failing to give them your communication and appropriate attention.

It is your ability to concentrate on the 20 percent, (not so much to disregard, discard the 80 percent) that often determines how far and fast you go. The top 20 percent of your patients will typically yield 80 percent of your professional satisfaction.

Here is a last 80/20 reality, the 20 percent of problems that are most difficult for you to solve have within them the possible solutions that can propel you to heights yet unimagined.

And it is the 20 of the 20 that are the most vexing and most valuable.

How To Increase Your Business 25-40 Percent Without Spending Another Dime

Your telephone is the one tool that opens or closes the door to your brick-and-mortar business. It must be handled with communication aplomb.

WHY?

* Nothing else matters if your phone is not answered well.

Handled well means prospective clients schedule and keep their appointments. Established patients keep their appointments. Just look at what happens if your phone is not answered well. The gate is closed. No marketing will matter.

When your marketing is handled well and your phone is answered well, you get the new clients you deserve. The gate is open.

So how well is your phone answered? How do you know? It is not necessarily by the present success of your business! It is not necessarily by the number of new clients!

Maybe your marketing is working so well that it has produced so many new clients that it has overcome your office's ability in answering the phone!

What to do—MEASURE. That which you measure, can improve. How do you measure?

* Keep a phone log. (Use just a plain spiral notebook. It need not be fancy.)
* Write down every call.
* Every call gets logged.
* Record the date, time, name of caller, caller's contact information, team member who took the call, result, dates for any follow-ups.

Today this log can be kept online or in your computer database. Moreover, recording each call and tracking its origin is relatively simple. Those recordings are invaluable in training your team, which has to communicate so well that callers virtually demand to become clients.

Look at the log. See what is happening. Track who does well on the calls. Who needs help? Train as needed. More training is better. Correct the team members that mess it up. Praise the ones who do it well.

* Create a written system for answering the phone.

Script the answers. Get the team members doing it well to train the others using the scripts. Once the team member learns the scripts well, answering well becomes second nature.

* Conduct telephone training.

Listen to them in the team meetings. Be sure to create answers to the questions that all new customers or clients are asking, if only to themselves: why should I choose you? Once you have the answers, practice with your team on giving the answers. Once your team knows that a mystery shopper is calling every so often, they will answer the calls better.

This Will Very Often Bring In More New Clients And Customers Without Spending

ANOTHER DIME. Some practices estimate a 25 percent to 40 percent increase from this alone.

The Five Critical Mistakes Almost Every Business and Professional Practice Makes

I am amazed sometimes at the ineptitude of practicing business owners in areas where they should know better.

Look over this list to see where you could improve. Note: it is the things you have omitted, the ones that you aren't doing—"The Nots"—that are the critical errors.

* Not figuring out what you are doing that is working.

When you are having success in your business or practice, you had better find out why…so you can continue to have the success. Just about everyone has had the experience of having a tremendous single month followed by a particularly down month. What happened is that the actions, ideas, concepts, etc. that created the great month were NOT continued, nor were they discovered, written down, or codified. Ouch! It is easier to continue what is working…if you know what it is.

* Not changing what isn't working.

When things aren't working as they should be, all too often, the owner "lets it ride" as though nothing can be done. I have never quite figured out the logic of this inaction… because it is illogical. It doesn't make any sense nor does it solve anything.

Problems left alone usually fester and worsen. The most often of these is the team member who continues to underperform and is left alone, all the while the business owner is hoping she/he will somehow quit.

If you think something is bad now, just wait to see what happens when you ignore it.

* Not recognizing that you are the creative energy and leader of your business.

When you take a break from your responsibility to be the inspirational leader and energy effuser for your business, business will decline.

Just watch how the team responds when you are less energetic, a little down, or upset. They will almost always mirror your attitude and viewpoint for that day.

Your practice or business will decline faster and further if you are the "do everything" kind of person who doesn't delegate. Funny thing is that the reason most often used to not delegate is "I want it done right."

Now, when you stop putting the energy into the practice, the energy needed isn't available from other sources, like your team or partners or associates. If you are going to lead, LEAD. Other people are counting on you.

* Not being a continuing student of your profession, both administratively and technically.

When you're not growing and expanding, it is virtually assured that the reason is not your knowledge of your profession. Yes, you do need continuing education, technically. Just remember that at least 50% of your success will be based on your skills and imple-mentation of leadership, strategy, planning, marketing, sales, per-sonnel, financial controls, and quality control.

Truthfully, many business people and professionals are just more comfortable in the technical arena. For a quick and easy reminder on where to focus your attention, ask yourself this question: "What matters most to my patients and team?" Many professionals are in a serious catch- up position to bring the non-clinical, non-technical administrative parts of their businesses up to the standards of their professional skills.

* And most serious, not continuing to do what is working.

When any particular course of action is working to bring about change and improvements, you would think that the individual would want to continue those actions. Not necessarily —to his/ her peril and very real loss.

The business person starts a program that results in increased production, more profit, more satisfaction, more time off, or some other benefit, and then quits the course of action that helped to create that improvement or positive change in the first place. Any outsider looking in would scratch his head, say, "Gee whiz, that wasn't very smart," and wonder why someone would stop.

It isn't rational. But professionals do it all the time. It is either ignorance or self-defeating behavior or success that is outrunning the sense of self-worth that would cause them to stop. This is what others might call stupid.

When something is working, just continue to do it!

Do find out how to add to it. You'll often get an even better result. This happens with everything you do. It is wisdom when you can learn from others who have made the mistakes you don't want to make and learn from their successes too. Be wise—learn from the smart man's experience.

Offense and Defense

Whether it is the NFL or college basketball or any other sport, have you noticed that the winning teams were a combination of offense and defense, playing as a team to win? Yes, they went to their stars in moments of "crunch time." This is nothing more than playing to their strengths. Give the ball to the players who can get it done.

* What are your strengths that allow you to "get it done"?

There is no such championship in business. But the necessity of scoring (producing and collecting) and playing defense (controlling your expenditures) still holds true.

All the great teams in sports play both offense and defense. Likewise, so do businesses, of all kinds and sizes, play offense and defense.

The winners are those who play the game very well. Championships are made from playing both well. How do you play the game? Do you have a defensive focus or are you more offensive-minded?

* You can win with a focus or strength in either one, but you must play both, even if you are better at one than the other.

You maximize your profit by playing defense (conserving your money) and by playing offense (increasing your productivity and collection). What kind of professional are you? How do you like to play the game?

If you are defensive-minded, your opportunity lies in learning to play a better offense—learn how to make more money as a business through various income centers and often additional services. This means either offering new services or doing a lot more of what is productive and profitable.

Interestingly, some professionals ignore or simply don't know about the various income centers that could provide additional income!

As an individual, how can you increase your personal productivity on an hourly basis? What services could you offer that will get you that needed boost in hourly productivity?

Sometimes the problem lies with not spending enough to open up the production to new levels. This is an example of overemphasizing the defensive aspect of your game. You can also overemphasize offense.

If you are already good on offense, your greatest possibilities lie in learning how to conserve and control your spending. Often, the most potent producers have the hardest time with learning to economize. What could you do without? What spending could you avoid? What resources could you better utilize with the net effect of decreasing your costs?

Do you really need that latest technological whiz-bang? Look, I have lots of them. It is just important to know how you will turn that piece of equipment into profitable increased productivity before you buy. And if you have already bought it, executing a plan that ensures it does make you more money.

Winning

"Winning isn't everything. The will to prepare to win is everything."
- Vince Lombardi

If you are like me, you have heard the other statement given as a quote. You know the one: "Winning isn't everything, it is the only thing." Well, that isn't what was said.

On a recent teleconference, one of the speakers, Joe Camp, corrected the quote. He was there when Lombardi gave a talk to one of the Ohio State football teams of Woody Hayes.

There is a big difference.

Few business owners and few people PREPARE enough to win—to ensure winning.

Preparing takes work. It takes time. It takes energy. It takes knowing the right thing to do. Knowing the right thing to do is the x factor that propels you to greater success even if you do no more than you are already doing.

Many dentists are unwilling to do the preparation or, at least, supervise the preparation done by someone else to ensure they win. A win here means to achieve some goal or some condition of satisfaction.

Preparation failure usually shows itself in a lack of coordinated strategy, lack of weekly statistical reports, and a lack of interpreting what those reports mean. It shows itself in results you fail to achieve.

Preparation is about planning to do whatever it takes to get the job done. Preparation is about considering the future and what it will take to make your future, the one you want to have. Creating the targets or goals is a major part of preparation. It is hard to prepare for something unknown.

If you don't know what you are shooting for, it is hard to hit it. Have you ever played the game of blind archery? You don't know what you will hit, but it is sure to create a ruckus!

Consider how you are preparing for each year, month, week, and day so you are ready and can get what you want. Make a commitment to prepare better. It takes some doing. And when you do it, you will take a huge load off. Most of your stress will dissolve… and you'll feel so much better about yourself.

Definitely prepare yourself so you can assume the position of leadership so necessary for successful patient interaction. How well you connect with patients and team is determined by your emotional awareness and skills. Your emotional intelligence is critical. Have you honed yours?

A Simple Success Strategy

This is so simple, but so overlooked. I could say it is just stupid and irrational to stop what is working. I could say it is self-defeating to stop what is working. I could say it is laziness. How about the excuse "it just seemed the right idea at the time?" I could say it is unthinking. But I won't. I will let you come to your own conclusions.

If the action you are taking is successful, keep doing it. Yes, you must be aware of changing circumstances. Yes, you must be aware of any sign of the action becoming less successful. Yes, it is prudent to tinker in small ways with the action to see if you can get an even better result. But don't stop what you know works!

Examples:

You used to call and check on patients who had major work done. Clients loved it. You got busy. Your practice or business was booming. Suddenly you didn't have time for this huge practice satisfaction builder and just stopped calling.

You used to write personal notes to all your new patients and those who referred them. It didn't take long. In fact, it took less time to write the notes than the time you took browsing a magazine or checking your email box full of spam. But again you stopped. "I am just too busy to do those anymore."

You used to take some time to get to know your patients and keep a relationship log of important personal items to relate to when dealing with them the next time. It took hardly any extra time.

You just did it while normally talking to the person, as you would go about your typical procedures. Never mind that the client's face would light up and spirits zoom when you talked about their kids or grandkids. But you stopped.

The reasons you stopped do not matter. Just start again. And make sure you continue what is working presently.

Take this as a wake-up call. You deserve great success for all that you do—success that should come to you both professionally and personally. The book you are reading right now is designed specifically for this reason—to ensure that you get the success you deserve.

Unfortunately, success is not bestowed. It is earned and unearned continuously. Here is what to do:

* Find out what is working. Write down these successful actions. Look high and low.
* Look at everything: patients, personnel, promotions, profits, management, leadership, business principles, people principles, and your own development as a leader, manager, marketer, persuader and professional. Include the actions you are now taking and the ones you used to do.
* Keep doing what is working.
* Determine consciously which actions you want to continue or revive. Insert these into your routines and calendars.

* Re-check from time to time to see what has dropped out. Put the successful actions back in.
* Find new things that work. Find new successful actions, methods, models, systems, behaviors, and processes. Every business/practice (and person) is on a journey of im-provement. That is what makes life and practice new and satisfying.

How You Think

Lessons of the Little Green Worm

She is bigger than he is. How much bigger? So much bigger that he was originally thought to be a parasite that lived inside her. She is 200,000 times bigger than him.

Whoa Nellie. The sex life of the green spoon worm is certainly unique. He lives inside of her reproductive tract, regurgitating sperm over the course of his short life—two months. Talk about a sex slave! She lives for about two years in the cracks of the sea floor.

Without him, the species disappears. Strangely, he has the same basic genetic code within him as she does. What determines the sex of the green spoon worm is what sex the larva meets in the first three weeks of existence. If it meets a female, the larva becomes a male and is committed to a life of sperm regurgitation.

If around a male, the larva becomes a she. What has this got to do with you and your practice success?! Far more than you realize. Little things do matter.

Would you have ever thought that something so small could have such a big effect?

Your case presentation is certainly subject to the axiom that little things do matter. The smallest thing (to you) can set a patient on the course of yes… or no.

While it is impossible to account for every little thing, the better you do, the better off you'll be when it comes to influencing people to make choices for their own good.

There are three areas that come to mind right away.

* Cultural Mores

Every culture has its "rules"—spoken and unspoken. If you violate these general rules, you'll be shunned or ostracized. These include appearance, manners, speech, dress, politics, education, and pursuits of work and play.

Naturally, there are variants, subcultures, and exceptions. Many celebrities deliberately break these rules to get attention. Lady Gaga, Paris Hilton, and Kim Kardashian come to mind in present times.

While some celebrities can break these rules, professionals cannot do so with impunity. As a professional, your patients expect a certain look, behavior, and excellence of the educated.

Violations such as going barefoot or having an office that looks and smells like a bar will kill your business or prevent it from ever getting started.

Looking like a professional and behaving like one is important to the confidence your clients have in you. It is the reality they need to give you their trust. "Too professional," on the other hand, is a client turn-off.

Being a human professional genuinely interested in the client is always professional. It is the little things, the trifles that matter far more than you realize.

* Being Different

For clients to choose you, they need reasons why they should. Your duty is to communicate this. The weakest possible reasons are because you are geographically close and/or otherwise convenient.

You would not refuse them as patients but you had better ensure they know what sets you apart from the rest of the available choices once you are chosen.

Strangely, too many dentists do not really have a definition of what sets them apart from the rest.

How can a patient decide you are different if you don't demonstrate it, show it, tell it, live it?

* What you say and do matters a lot.

In a professional service business, for example, you count far more than in any other business.

Your communication is sought and valued because of your status. Use it wisely. The smallest error or omission can be a detriment. This is not something to agonize over.

The easiest ways to stay on track are:

* Use good manners
* Do "the little things" that others omit
* What the patient tells you -listen

This is a major, major omission for 95 percent of dentists. This isn't a blame. You are busy, sometimes very busy. Still, one of the most important facets of the relationship you have with your clients is the quality of your listening.

Two Helps with Listening:

* **Compartmentalize Your Time** - With most clients, you should compartmentalize the time and focus on listening intently. The best way to do this is to ask directed questions that give you the answers you need.
* **Set a Time Limit** - This can be just for you or announced to the patient. When you focus your attention, you will not need as much time to transfer the feeling to the patient that you are really listening. With consultations that you are giving gratis, it is important to set the time frame at the beginning, for patients will often milk you for as much as they can if given the opportunity to do it for free. Attorneys are an excellent model to follow with time: if you take it, you pay for it. Legal clients very quickly learn that chit chat can be expensive. Put a fifteen-minute limit on your time during a free consultation and stick to it.

Have you ever heard a person complain, "My [anything] listens too much?" If you're going to err with listening, do so on the side of ample. More listening is the mistake you can afford to make. Listening is difficult to titrate to some mythical optimum.

It is a little thing to listen well, just as the male green spoon worm is little, but without that little thing, your practice is barred from the growth that could occur.

Humans need those little things.

In what areas do you need to consider the power of the little green worm? Little things do matter.

Breaking Down the Boxes

I remember those liquor boxes oh so well. At the time, I was twenty-three years old and glad to have a job for the summer between the first and second years of dental school.

There I was, working as a stock "person" and cashier in one of the state-run ABC liquor stores in Richmond, Virginia. The manager there could have been my grandfather. He had been there thirty-five years. This was his last year.

He showed me how to break down all the liquor and wine boxes. He deftly wielded the box knife as a chef does his favorite paring knife, fast and seemingly without much effort. He broke down the box in nothing flat.

"This looks easy," I thought to myself. "Why is he spending so much time showing me how to break down a box?" I wondered silently.

"Maybe there is more to it than I am thinking," was my answer. Well, I was right. It was far more challenging than I thought. It was physically demanding. Some of those boxes had double and triple bottoms to support the weight of the bottles. My hands got tired, and quick. It wasn't my favorite task.

Every day we had to break down the boxes, otherwise, they would overwhelm the dumpster quickly.

I don't miss them at all.

Now I deal with an entirely different set of boxes. Mental ones carefully constructed to create a winning solution to a problem. When they were originally conceived and workable, they were wonderful. The problem with mental boxes, as well as physical ones, is that they outlive their usefulness.

So what is it about the mental box that is so darn tough?

People protect their boxes. I mean they will attack you if you try to take them away. These boxes can be seen as security, as the winning answer when there were no others, as the solution that has evaded everyone else.

The problems with the boxes (and thinking inside that once-valid box) are that they are dated and out of touch with now.

At one point in time, the sailing ship was the transportation of choice solution for getting to Asia. The trip could take months. It was a good solution then.

Today, you would question the sanity of a person who opted to take a slow boat to China when he could get there within a day.

Here is a little trick to open up and begin the breakdown of the toughest boxes. It is how I think about all mental constructed boxes.

Most people look at that box as having four sides, a bottom, and a top. It is one neat package of a problem and its solution wrapped up together within that box. My basis of operation is to take the top off the box right away. I question the validity of every box.

Let me encourage you to look at the box as being topless. A topless box. That way you can see what the walls and bottom are made of, if you will just look.

A more ambitious approach is to question each wall of the box. I call this zero-based thinking. This is named after the concept of zero-based budgeting where every expenditure is questioned and none is accepted as a given.

Look at the box from every angle, inside and out. What does each one contain that is accepted as "truth"? What was once "true" that is not any longer?

Is the "truth" always true? Is the "truth" malleable?

Are you using a "truth" to justify a position you are taking?

Is something now true that once was not, that should be added to create a new solution? Are you using a "truth" to stop moving forward because you are fat and happy where you are?

It is the fat and happy that are subject to the disruptive innovations that can shake an industry. They become the skinny and depressed when it hits them.

Now here comes the zero-based part: what if you declared everything up for grabs? What if you dropped all premises and acted as if they did not exist?

Dell Computer changed the sales of computers by going directly to the consumer.

Every computer was customized to the requests of the future user. They changed their factories to include their suppliers.

Their suppliers are physically located at the same place as the factory, to deliver supplies just in time as they are needed. Profitability soared as inventory costs dwindled to unheard of ranges. It certainly didn't hurt that Dell had advanced systems in place to take advantage of eCommerce. They get paid in advance before the computer is built!

Dell re-wrote the rules by which every other computer company worked. It became, at the time, the largest PC company in the world, and put several billion dollars in Michael Dell's pocket for a time.

Dell changed the game by instituting new processes of market-ing, selling, and building computers. The computers are pretty much like everyone else's. Yet, the zero-based thinking of "what if we…" changed the entire industry.

This sort of disruptive innovation will occur again and again—innovation based on zero-based thinking, where virtually nothing is held as set in stone.

If your product or service is perceived as being virtually the same as everyone else's, you need to find some strategic differentiator. The other choice is to compete in a crowded field where everyone is thought of as about the same, and pricing is based on supply and demand…just like commodities.

What could you change about the process of your service or product that gives you strategic advantage over your competitors?

Today, Dell has fallen behind because the marketplace has changed and they have not.

Governor

I was driving that go-cart for all it was worth. It just wouldn't go any faster. I still remember the frustration of trying to go faster. No matter how hard I pressed the pedal, it would not go any faster.

Pedal to the metal and nothing more could be extracted from that darn thing. My son had cleverly managed to get ahead of me and was blocking every angle of getting by him. I could almost hear him smirking inside—that special one that every son at age fourteen enjoys when he gets ahead of his dad.

My go-cart had a governor. It could go faster, a lot faster, enough for me to win. It had a little set screw that prevented more gas from going into the carburetor. No more gas, no more speed. It was limited by a mechanical device.

People do not have a mechanical set screw that limits their "gas." People have a belief system instead. And it is far larger and more difficult to dislodge, change, or remove than any set screw. It helps you win or it stops you dead, right where you are.

This belief system is so powerful that it will repulse all attempts to overcome even when it is known. No matter how much one knows that the belief system is the limiting factor, it is the ruler of the roost.

It will foil all attempts to get around it. It will hide chameleon-like when challenged. It will provide the little voice inside your mind that says it is not there. It will confound any logical attempt to eradicate it.

When one does not value himself or the value of what one does highly enough, it will put the brake on any advancement. This can be a tough pill to swallow…and it is the truth.

It doesn't matter how good or advanced the advice and tools you use are if you are unconsciously preventing their successful applications from working. I see it happen all the time.

How do you know you have limiting beliefs?

If you are not getting what you want, in spite of efforts and actions that have proven successful elsewhere, then look to the results to see if you have limiting beliefs.

If others using them are producing the results desired, then you are either using them incorrectly or committing self-sabotage. Look. Examine. If you are using them as directed, you may have limiting beliefs.

It requires an entire mental re-framing to overcome.

Beliefs and behaviors must be congruent. One supports the other. When you find that your actions do not match your beliefs, you will invariably revert to your beliefs. There are dozens of ways to trip yourself up.

One very common way is to take a workable application, technique, ad, or system and leave a part or several pieces out. The thinking will go like:

"I didn't need that part." Or "I don't have time to do it that way." Or "I'll improve the system by changing it to my way." Or-or-or.

Yeah, right!

Whether learning a new technique or using a new application, first use it as designed. Emulate before you create.

Once you are successfully using it as designed and understand how and why it works, then you can start to add your improvements or take parts away to streamline it. Anything else is gambling and the odds are against you.

When you see this written down on paper, its clarity blazes across the page like a giant searchlight of truth. It is easy to see in others.

When it comes to real life, it strikes at the little set screws of success limitation that most have carefully placed to justify their station in life.

You will only allow yourself to be as successful as your governor will allow. One could say that one does screw oneself!

The first step to removing the governing set screws is to find the ones you have. This is the toughest part. They hide, confuse, and refuse to be found. They do not want to be found out or removed. Persist. These leeches on your life bleed you of success and the joys of it.

The second step is to examine the value of each limiting belief. This requires a disciplined approach to rational evaluation. The beliefs once served you in some way. Most are out of date.

The ugliest and most painful are the ones that you use to blame others for your life. Victimhood rings stronger and stronger in our society. Many exploit and blame others for their station in life. The news is filled with stories of victims.

It is easier to be a victim than to take responsibility for results in one's life. The sad truth is that blaming others brings no solution—only an excuse. Excuses do not solve problems. When you blame someone else for your failure, you are closing the door on your own choices and your own responsibilities for your success.

An Ugly Picture

The third and final step is to decide which beliefs serve you and which ones stop you. Then choose the ones that support your real values and intentions.

Consider this very important principle: you matter. What you do does make a difference.

Here is the second guiding principle: you have a responsibility to be successful. You cannot help others become better if you are not in a position to do so. If you barely have enough, it is hard to give to others.

The third principle is contributism. Decide to make a difference for someone or many someones. Find a cause you believe in and support it in spades. There is a deep and abiding joy in helping. You are in a position to make a difference for so many. First, make a difference for yourself.

Clarity of Purpose - Begin with the End in Mind

If all the fears we have as human beings, one of the worst is being afraid to name what we want in life.Many people are reluctant to fully describe the life they want to lead, the feelings they want to experience.

Indeed, it is rare for anyone to FULLY describe the ideal life for themselves.

Why is this true? Because that life, the ideal life, is one that is so valuable that it would be so painful to declare it and then not achieve it.

Having never named it, the individual is spared the pain of failing to achieve it. Additionally, and maybe more importantly, the individual feels as if he doesn't deserve to have that life.

The question is: who makes the rules? Who decides who deserves? YOU DO.

Yes, there are societal rules created for the good of its members, but these do not block the creation of the life you want to live. No, the person who blocks that ideal life is you, if only accidentally. If this is a shock, well, I am glad you were awakened. Now that you are awake, why not go ahead and describe that ideal life of yours!

Describe what you want out of life. Pretend that the money needed for that life is not in question for now.

Describe the pay of living that you will enjoy in your life as a result of what you do. Describe your normal day. Paint the picture of your life just as you want it. Describe your activities, who you are sharing it with, where you live, where you want to go.

The difficulty in doing this is the disbelief that it is possible. Suspend your disbelief for now.

Be CLEAR. Define that ideal life. It is difficult to go from where you are to another place unless it is named without ambiguity. Can you imagine how difficult it would be to get to your unknown place from where you currently live? It is VERY hard to get to an end point unless you know where it is!

BE SPECIFIC. Name it. Describe it. Detail it. Detail it some more. Now detail it some more still. Just be sure it is what you want. IF it is your true desire, you will be energized to talk about it. You can have it. Getting there is the fun of living, if you know where you are going. Begin with your end in mind.

Read this several times. Summon up the courage to do this. You make the rules.

Risk, Change, and the Joy of the Learned Hare

All progress comes from taking a risk to make a change. These two, risk and change, are commonly confused. They are not the same. Change can have varying amounts of risk, from picayune to ginormous.

The irony is that making no change eventually becomes the riskiest act of all. Companies and individuals aren't really different because companies are composed of people, subject to the vagaries, vices, and virtues of human nature.

What drives the no-change approach to business and professional practices? Success.

What! That's right, success.

When what you are doing is working, why change? Why take the risk of messing up a good thing? Why change a system or service or product that is making a lot of profit?

Ask General Motors. Ask U.S. Steel. Ask the buggy whip manufacturers. Ask the typewriter producer.

It is ironic that Henry Ford borrowed the technique of assembly line manufacturing from the meatpacking plants of Chicago to create an assembly line built car that virtually every person in America could buy.

Before he came along there were over two thousand custom car makers, all making them one at a time at a cost out of reach for the common man.

You could get a car from Ford in any color you liked...as long as it was black. Later, Ford, the most innovative car producer in the early 1900s, was surpassed by General Motors as the world's biggest car maker in the 1920s, precisely because it would not change!

Some of the most successful companies ever became that way simply because the existing competition did not change. The risk-takers re-wrote the rules for success.

Has it ever occurred to you why companies have a finite life? Why aren't companies hundreds of years old? You would think that at least a few would adapt themselves and still be around! How many can you think of that still remain?

Often the original founder of an enterprise wills success beyond what the average man believes possible. He constantly studies what works and adapts his company to the breezes, gusts, and hurricane force winds that inevitably wend their way into the path of all companies.

Once that brilliant force of adaptive change is gone, the company often begins a slow but inexorable decline.

Sam Walton created a company that has become the world's largest retailer. The long-term question is can it continue to adapt and change without the wisdom of Sam, the wizard of retail discount pricing? He was an individual who took risks and made them a force for profit. You can, too.

What about individuals? Does this "stuck in the past" mode that was once successful occur here too? Yep.

Change is the only assured condition. Yet success seduces those who experience it to believe what made them successful before will continue to do so…forever. Be it hope or haughtiness of prior winning, or laziness or pride, this seduction leaves its owner bewildered when others pass them by.

Nothing stays the same. So the greatest risk of all is refusing to take any. So now what? Once you embrace change as your partner rather than your enemy, you can move forward. Not storming forward headlong, but wisely, to risk change the right way.

Five Principles of Turning Risk Into Reward

Know your risk quotient

Everyone has a different comfort zone with risk. You should recognize yours. For many, change and risk are relished, others abhor them. Neither is completely right or wrong. If you tend toward the No Change-No Risk Zone, recognize that no change is the riskiest of all.

Second, understand that if an idea makes you a touch uncomfortable—that is a good thing. No progress is made at all without some change. You weren't comfortable the first time you learned anything, whether it was the first time you hit a golf ball, asked someone out for a date, or went to a job interview. The stretch for you as a little to no change person doesn't have to be wild and crazy—just a stretch. As you discover that it is OK to change, you will find the bit of risk to be a good thing.

The other side of the risk coin, willingness to take virtually any risk, to change anything and everything at will is as bad, and possibly worse, than "Mr. No Change." Every risk you take has to have an upside that is worth the downside you could endure. In other words, what is a reasonable tolerance for risk? The answer is that it depends on your situation.

To risk everything is usually unwise. Just as one diversifies his risk by investing in multiple stocks, real estate, etc., so too does one diversify his risk by not allowing one thing that could go wrong disrupt the entire applecart.

Sure, many have taken big risks and won. So too, have many taken big risks and lost.

It is OK to risk a lot when one is younger or has less to lose, because you have time to make it up. But as your financial success increases, your tolerance for financial risk decreases—or it should.

Just as the smart gambler puts a stop loss on how much he is willing to lose, so too should a smart player take financial chips off the table out of potential harm's way once he has achieved some financial success.

Entrepreneurs are typically perfectly willing to tolerate risks that most others are not willing to take. That makes them who they are. If you are entrepreneurial, recognize that others "can't think with you" and won't risk what you will.

That's all right too. That alone gives you an edge. Still, you shouldn't dive out of the plane and build your parachute on the way down. Smart risking takes more than that.

Beware the call of the no-change crowd. If everyone listened to them, so little progress would be made that our society would inch along. That isn't the society we live in. Taking the go-slow approach is like doing the speed limit on the interstate—you are going to get run over.

Personally, I have failed many times. My job is to learn from the experience and not make the same mistake twice, while also learning what risks do make sense. Nothing ventured leads to no gain. Gain is the heartbeat of successful change.

The speed of change in your industry often dictates how fast you need to change. Now it is the fast that are eating the slow.

The hare wins these days, even as we celebrate the tortoise virtues of persistence and dogged tenacity. These days, the hare has learned from the tortoise and uses his speed!

* Mitigate risk

Smart risking means you find every way possible to remove unnecessary risks! How? By gathering data, research, and information. Find the worst that could happen and look to see if that is a tolerable result. If not, how could the potential losses be lessened? If they can't be lessened, next!

Look for others who have faced similar opportunity and risks. Look inside and outside your field. You typically won't find it inside your field. You will usually have to go outside it.

Ask:

* What happened?
* Did the risk-taker play it smart and still lose?
* What worked?
* What was missing?
* What could have been done to lessen the loss?
* What could have made it more successful?
* What key resource made it work?
* What key person made it work?
* If there was a problem, in what arena—finance, marketing, strategy, etc.?

Buy expert help. Consultants can be found to help you get what you need. It is foolish to be cheap with help that can mean the difference between over-the-top success and failure. The average person goes cheap and reaps the cheap rewards.

Figure how many blocks of risks an endeavor is worth. What is the upside? Are the downside risks worth it? You only have so much time, effort, and energy to use for the new. Leverage it the best you can by letting lesser opportunities go.

At some point, the opportunities can come at you so fast and appear so tantalizing as to give you Opportunity Intoxication. Don't get caught with your entrepreneurial blood level over the limit. Bankers and lawyers are standing by to pull you over and take your license for success.

Every new venture has within it opportunity costs.

If you place your time, energy, and efforts into this one new thing, what will it cost you in other areas where your skills and talents have proven themselves? Is the "new thingy" worth the potential losses in what you know works?

Do you have the time to devote to the new thingy? Where will you steal time? Will you drop something else to make time? Will you take the time out of your family or self-time? What would happen if the same money were placed into other investments? Where would the return be better?

Beware the lure of the new with its siren call to lay aside other parts of your life. The next new thingy is often just bright and shiny while being no better, and often worse, than what you have going on right now.

On the other hand, if the risk is changing your existing business or practice so it can advance, then another analysis is appropriate. Is the program successful with others? Does the program make sense? Is the teacher/ mentor/coach someone with a proven record of accomplishment of helping? Is the program based on real world experience and results?

I am not anti-risk about taking on new things. I take on a lot. These days I pass up more than I take. Some entrepreneurial types go head long from one "can't lose" thing to the next. Usually that person is better off weighing the pros and cons more studiously and passing on all but the best and most opportune.

Some need to get more adventuresome. Use these questions to decrease the risks and know what you are getting yourself into.

* Think like a chess player

Successful chess players have one common characteristic that helps them play to win. This characteristic is ingrained into all winning players.

What is it? Think many moves ahead. The further ahead one can think, the more comfort that can be had in playing the game of risk. Unlike chess, your game of risk typically has no one named opponent.

Instead, the game of risk has your seven soldiers of success required to conquer the foes and win the game: mindset, people, strategy, PR, marketing, sales, and finances. Each soldier must be given sufficient rations and led with cleverness to win not only the early battles but also all the future ones that are part of the game.

Not all battles must be won to win, just the most important ones.

Inherent within this thinking is contingency planning. This is the classic "what if " game that determines readiness to match whatever comes your way. This is one of the more unpopular ways of thinking as one must squarely face his risks head on.

It has been said that if an entrepreneur knew what he would need to endure to overcome all the barriers, frustrations, and snafus, he would have never begun!

Still, it is foolhardy to begin with only one eye open. As well as risk, there are also enormous opportunities. Some come your way through sheer serendipity, others from concentrated effort to find them. When you are aware of the possible risks and opportunities, you can move with speed to do what you need to do when you need to do it. Are you ready?

* Go with your educated gut.

You can't know everything before you act.

When asked, CEOs of major corporations told researchers that most often, when asked for a decision, that they went with their gut. Understand that their gut is a very educated and experienced gut that has been through alot, had multiple mentors, extensive schooling, and all manners of business research available to them. Still when not all the factors can be known, you have to go with what feels right.

Some analytical types cringe at this idea. But the question remains, when everything cannot be known beforehand, how does one make a wise decision? When it is impossible to have all the data before you decide and act, you have to act still. Realize that not deciding is a form of deciding itself.

General George S. Patton of the U.S. Army and Hollywood movie fame is reported to have said that a good plan done now is better than a perfect plan done one week from now. He understood that speed was an important part of winning.

Unnecessary delays can cause your side to lose an opportunity, if not compromise the success of your venture. Speed has become one of the new imperatives of success.

Going with your gut is often the only way to decide when facts and data are incomplete. It is useless to vacillate back and forth when the unknown cannot be brought to light. Listen to the decision inside and go with that.

* Know when to look for risk.

When you are doing well, and I mean really well, the allure is to ignore any and all calls to change anything. It is human nature to be this way. It is also the downfall of some very bright people who think they are above the calls for change from consumers and users.

What should you do?

Keep doing what is working. Augment it. Strengthen it. And... use your Research and Development to start looking at how your present approach could be usurped.

Your R&D looks for the chink in your armor that could give your competitors in the marketplace an advantage that you cannot match. Your R&D is always looking to find the next big thing and prevent you from being left out, profitless, and pitiful.

You can't afford to make this a huge part of your budget unless you are already far behind. No, it should be a small percentage of expenditures to reliably put you where your competitors can't catch up. Think of this like spending money for insurance. You hope you never need it, but when you do, you are really glad you got it.

Your R&D needs some of your attention and certainly your encouragement. For most small businesses and practices, this means that the owner must go snooping around, breathe in the societal trends, and keep up with the latest and greatest from not only his field, but similar ones also. He has to be "in the know" about the culture, newest trends, and probable futures.

Another R&D imperative occurs when your present situation is not as successful as it should be. Then you are simply looking for a resource, guide, coach, or anyone that can help you get where you want to go.

Throughout all of this, it's important to keep doing what is working while listening to the voice of the marketplace in two ways. First, what they say they want. Second, what they would want if it were available.

This is a riskier and still predictable way to stay ahead of the competitive curve. Why? Because it's based on human wants, needs, desires, and human nature. Tap into these and risk melts away as the profit piles up.

How You Charge

How Do You Charge More and Have Your Clients, Customers, Guests, Patrons, and Patients Love It?

Sounds like a great idea, doesn't it? It's what we all dream about, yet it's a bit counterintuitive, isn't it? Well, it's possible. Actually, not only is it possible, it's the right thing for you to do.

Let's talk first about charging more as a concept.

Everybody, in order to be successful, is going to have to work hard. That's just the way it is. Still, if you've got to work hard, isn't it better to leverage your work to produce more results per unit of time and effort? I thought you'd agree.

The goal of this material is to help you create more time and make more money and reap the benefits and fruits of your efforts and work. Too many work too hard for too little. If you're in that group, you need to listen up and listen big, because you're about to learn some things that are quite different.

These things are outside the regular thinking and quite outside the box. In fact, it's a whole new universe. If all this sounds good, let me help show you the lay of the land. First, remember this axiom: if it was easy, everyone would do it. So, expect difficulty.

The road to success is messy. Expect a mess. Anyone who tries to do something new or tries to discover what's going on without expecting some type of mess is in for a rude awakening. There are hills and valleys and bumps and bruises that you're going to have to endure, and frankly, it is part of the journey.

Second, understand that for you to learn how to charge more and have your clients love it, it's kind of like climbing Mount Everest. Even if you're an experienced mountain climber, you still want an experienced guide who's been there, done that.

No matter how much talent, work ethic, smarts, ability, and knowledge you have, you'll need someone who can lead you past the pitfalls. You'll need someone who can lead you along the narrow paths and up the hill with the least danger possible to you so you achieve your goals.

Third, remember it's a journey. You'll make mistakes, even with a guide. The important thing to do is to 'fail' forward, to minimize the losses and to exacerbate the gains. All too commonly, we take our losses and magnify those.

What child hasn't experienced the parent who looks at the C in the whole gaggle of A's and says, "What happened?" instead of congratulating the A's.

We have to think outside the parameters of human nature a bit. Don't worry, I'm here to help you out. So, let's begin.

What are the components of the philosophy of successful business? Well, there are many of them. Let's start with the first one. It's mindset. How do you consider yourself, your company, and your practice? What is your view of the business environment? Is it a positive-sum game or a zero-sum game?

I come down squarely on the positive side, with a ringing thud, a clang of the anvils saying, "We're the positive side."

Let me explain.

If you think that there's only so much success to go around, you'll be in a constant battle as a competitor instead of a collaborator. In reality, there's lots of success to go around. The zero-sum game is proposed by those who are a bit cynical. Skeptical of what's possible.

Now, there is a difference between a skeptic and a cynic. A cynic sees the bad and has little room for the good. A skeptic says, "Prove it to me and maybe I'll accept it." There's a difference.

So, the first thing is your mindset, how you think about things and about possibilities.

Amongst those is this mindset: who you are and who's your client. It's something to always keep in mind. Who you are and who's your client. The first place that most people start is with who they are and what they do, and then look for a market. The reality is to find the market—your Who—or as I say, "Who's your Who?" and then find ways to give them offerings that meet their wants and needs.

On to strategy: strategy is the overarching plan of how to overcome the noise of other marketing to present you and your offerings in a unique way that makes your Who, your market, want what you've got.

Most small businesses and practices are strategy-less. They haven't really considered one. "I'm just a 'blank.'" "I'm only an attorney." "I'm only a dentist." "I'm only a small building contractor." It doesn't matter.

Not having a strategy is basing your whole system of your business on hope. And hope just isn't a good strategy.

So, accept the fact that you need a strategy. You'll be more effective in your marketplace. It will save you energy, time, and money, and it declares what you aren't. You see, the moment you declare what you are, you are going to naturally attract certain clients, customers, patrons, patients, or guests to what you have. But you also turn away and reject those that don't match up.

For this you should clap your hands and dance a jig because the reality is that's what you want. Trying to be everything to everybody is just asking for it. Think about it like this: attempting to appeal to everybody is like shooting a target with a blunderbuss.

You remember what those blunderbusses are? They're those huge shotgun-type rifles that sprayed widely, mostly ineffectively, versus a high-power rifle with a laser scope that narrows in exactly on your target.

That's the difference between having a strategy that makes a declaration and trying to appeal to everyone. Appealing to everyone typically means you're not appealing to anyone strongly.

So, what's next? Positioning. What is positioning, really? It's a combination of the thoughts, concepts, ideas, words, and mental images that are stored in the marketplace of your Who. Those who should be attracted to what you have to offer.

A "position" means you occupy a market space on the continuum of your offering. Example: "I'm the number one provider of computer software and training in my area." That's a position. It's positioning yourself as Number One. Another position: "We are the first to bring computer training to the area of Philadelphia." That's another position, being the first.

Another position: "We are the fastest to deliver your products and services to you at the time that you need them. You have a computer shut-down? We're there within an hour, and that's guaranteed." That would be an example of speed—we are the fastest. When a potential client thinks of what you have to offer, when you're properly positioned, they'll think of you.

You'll notice that most of the new products introduced in our marketplace are ones that try to create a category of one.

A great example of a category of one is the Cirque du Soleil. The circus/Broadway theater blend now made famous the world over. Their position is a category of one. Not circus, not play, not musical, but certainly a spectacle.

Further examples of position in the marketplace: you can be high-priced, like the Four Seasons Hotel. You can be low-priced, like Wal-Mart Stores. You can be speedy, like One Hour Photo or One Hour Cleaners, or FedEx. Of course, what is e-mail but high-speed mail? Created well, your position eliminates the wannabes.

It helps grease the skids and reduces the friction of the entire process of your client saying yes to you. Our next category is public relations—an overt plan to become known by the public by means other than traditional advertising.

It is composed of stories, articles, events, web-based initiatives, even product placements. The good news about public relations is that you can do it yourself. Most folks don't do it themselves because they haven't got the time, however, public relations can be accomplished by you or with a group, but it's more than just publicity.

Have you noticed all the products that now show up in movies that never used to be there? Those are purposeful public relations efforts. They are actually positioned so you see the brand name at the time that the movie is run.

These people aren't fools. They pay millions of dollars for that association. Remember that your public relations are about providing news, some "hook" that a reporter would want to have more information about.

And by the way, news outlets are looking for you and what possible news you can provide. They're not interested in promoting your practice or your business directly, but they are interested in providing news, things that people want to know about.

So, the key to using public relations is to become the go-to expert to make sure that you're doing enough of what I call "eventing." Providing events for people to attend that associate your name with those. And as our society changes, I want you to notice how frequent charitable participation in causes has become in the marketplace. In fact, it's growing in importance.

Our next arena is marketing. Everyone knows that you need it. Gone forever is the concept, "If I just do what I do well, I'll get all the referrals I need." Ha! Laughable, if it wasn't so sad. The reality is that if you put yourself up to getting referrals as the primary methodology of getting new clients, patrons, patients, guests, you are putting yourself at risk.

So, first accept the fact that you can't do it that way if you want to be successful. Are there situations where it's happened? Yes, there are. Typically such situations take place where the product or service or offering is so unique that people felt compelled to talk about it. There is a logic behind this, there's a system behind this possibility, but for most small businesses and practices, this isn't an option.

So, should one reject referrals as a methodology of marketing? Absolutely not. In fact, you should embrace it. But understand this: you have to do more than just hope for referrals. There's just too much noise out in the marketplace. People aren't as interested in referring. However, referrals do work. Most practitioners in small business are in the continuing saga of hoping for referrals.

If you want referrals, it has to be a planned system that's active, what I call the Optimum Referral Culture. That's for another day.

First, let's talk about three outstanding principles of marketing. Number one: it's part of a communication persuasion continuum which starts with "never heard of you" all the way up to active, rav-ing fan advocate. When you get someone who really has a fervent belief in what you do, they're going to tell other people.

How do you get the people to that point? It takes a bit of work. The second important principle about marketing is that effec-tive marketing never stops. It has to be consistent. In the market-place, only a small percentage of the public is interested in what you have to offer at any one time.

Furthermore, depending upon what you offer, the buying cycle could be longer or shorter than most. I'll give you an example. If you're a restaurant owner, you know that people have to eat every day, which means that your buying cycle is short.

If you run a furniture company, you know people don't buy furniture all that often (about every five years or so), so the buying cycle is much longer than the restaurant owner. You need to align your marketing plan with the length of the buying cycle of your Who, the people that buy from you.

The idea is to create long-term top-of-mind awareness that helps make the sale in the mind of your prospective client before he ever arrives in your business or practice. In fact, when it's done well, creating long-term top-of-mind awareness does up to 80 per-cent of the work of selling for you... Sounds good, doesn't it?

Let's talk about sales. Sales is the continuing process of communication that starts with public relations, goes through marketing, and finally into sales.

It's a continuing part of the process.

For those who follow the concepts here, selling for us is more like the un-sale. Most people think sales are about pushing a prospect into buying from you. No. It's about creating an attraction, what I call "pull marketing," where you create a mental environment inside your client in which he wants what you've got.

When you do that, you create two reinforcing pulls: your pull, and the pull that he gives. This virtually insures that he's buying. And that puts a smile on everyone's face, because you profit and your clients love the experience. Everybody wins.

Let's talk about experiences. This is the rising star in the world of commerce. The experience economy is upon us. The big challenge for the small business owner and professional is figuring out how to use it.

Experiences happen. Do you let them happen or do you make them happen? That is the key. Experience by design is a huge lever. When engineered well, it creates the grand pull. It happens when an experience is so unusual, surprising, positive, and delightful, and so noteworthy that word-of-mouth spreads like a virus for which there is no vaccine and no treatment. And that's a good thing!

Even an experience itself can become the marketing. Look no further than Disney World, Disneyland, the Disney Company. Disney was built on things that people want to experience. Disney helps create a positive memory that lasts a lifetime.

It's about families and about what happens in the minds and hearts of those who are there. It is a bit of a fantasy, but it's one that people enjoy. But it is a "want to." It's even called an attraction, isn't it?

Many companies and providers have an attractive offer. What if what you're offering is by nature a "don't want" offering? Then you've got problems.

And here's why. It's very difficult to get someone to buy something they don't want, isn't it? Well, I've got a little hint for you. No, it's not. Not when you design your marketing properly. What you're offering—is it something that your prospects naturally want?

Does your offering create a positive mental experience? Is it a positive emotional imprint that lasts, permeates, and activates future purchases of your offering? Hmm. Healthcare isn't one of those, is it? It's probably the largest category of offerings under the "don't want" group.

Do you want to have a vaccination? Doubt it. Do you want an exam where you're poked and prodded? Don't think so. Do you just want to have surgery, please? No. The "don't want" offerings are the ones that are the trickiest.

As a dentist, I understand this. When was the last time someone that you knew said, "Oh, goody, I get to go to the dentist!" Not gonna happen. It's just the way it is.

So, what are some of the want attraction-type of services? Restaurants. Travel and travel companies. Schools, although no one wants to take tests, they do want the education. Clothing. Beauty products. There's all kinds of lists of these.

You basically have two choices when you're a "don't want" provider. Number one: find a way to make your offering a "want" experience. In other words, change its character and nature so much so that people want to experience what you have.

As a sidebar here, remember this: the experience is defined in two different ways. If you're providing a personal service, it is going to be the experience of receiving it or the experience of using it.

And of course, the third category is the experience of receiving it and using it together. So, number one is find a way to make your offering a "want" experience. But number two is make sure your offering is better than putting up with the "don't want" condition or situation. Let me give you an example.

Nobody wants to have the roof repaired. But they do want to have a dry house. If you have a leaky roof, you're willing to put up with the experience of not wanting the roof to be leaking and pay the roofing company to make sure you can stay warm and dry inside your home.

It is important to understand that experiences can be planned to create emotion and to actually emote positive feelings, and should be designed this way. This is called staging and does take some extra effort, but the results can be extraordinary, both for you, your satisfaction with what you do, and the profit you provide for your client, because in truth you are giving them personal profit as they exchange money for your offering.

And, it can make a change in how your own team looks at what you do. My opinion of the relatively lukewarm reception of the experience economy has been that most people think of it as more work with no more dollars.

Well, I'm here to tell you, that isn't how it is.

The key to changing the experience equation is to create happy patients who want what you have and willingly pay your fee.

Fees, Appearances, and Expectations

How Does Price Affect Your Appreciation?

In a fascinating experiment, researchers at Cal Tech and Stanford used the MRI to monitor the responses in the brain to differently priced wines.

Their preferences based on pricing are illuminating.

The wines that were marked as higher priced stimulated the pleasure centers in the brain more than those marked as being lower priced. Even when the same wine was tested twice, once with a higher and then a lower price, the higher priced version was perceived as "better."

The pleasure centers of the brain "lit up" when the subjects in the experiment knew they were sampling the wine with the allegedly more expensive price tag.

One could say that the experience in the brain is altered when you are paying more for a product or service.

In Robert Cialdini's book Influence: The Psychology of Persuasion, he tells a story about a tourist jewelry shop. The turquoise bracelets and beads weren't selling. The shop owner sent a note to mark the jewelry at half price. One of the clerks mistakenly posted the turquoise at double the price! It all sold out within the hour.

Why this occurred could be associated with the perception of value. When the price seemed consistent with the perceived value of the jewelry, it sold. Perception and expectation matched.

Do Appearances Matter?

The restaurant was five stars. White tablecloths, crystal, and real silverware were arrayed carefully. The atmosphere was one of quiet elegance. The lighting was just right as the tuxedoed wait staff hovered close by, always ready without interfering with the guests' experience. When the food arrived, the plate was decorated with swirls of color in a lovely pattern.

It was simply a beautiful presentation—it was almost a shame to eat it. (I did anyway and yes, it was delicious.) The value was automatically elevated by the presentation. Fine restaurants know this. Even lesser ones decorate their plates with a bit of parsley to "give it some color."

Does this attention to aesthetics matter? Does it enhance the taste? Most people say yes. Given the choice of this level of attention to detail and appearance, which would be your choice? Back to our lessons from wines: in another experiment involving wines, the quality of the wine glasses made a difference! Cheap wine was found to taste better when presented in beautiful stemware. More expensive wine in cheap glasses was graded lower.

A Practical Lesson for You

When your fee is significantly higher than your competitors' fee, the whole experience, the whole perception of you and your ser-vice can be completely altered.

Still, it is important to differentiate your services from your competitors. It is vitally important for you to design the presentation and experience of your services to reinforce these differences. When you are able to do this, and you give your patient your best services, your patients will give you more positive comments and fewer negative ones.

People will automatically look for all the reasons why you and your services are worth it… and they are too.

The questions become: how can you use these lessons?

How could you apply these concepts to elevate the appreciation of the work you do? How does doing so help your client, too?

INNOVATION

The Rifled Musket, Drowning in Your Own Success, and A Union Saved

History. That's the subject that teaches lessons from the past for today. And a misunderstanding of applying its principles cast Gettysburg's Civil War fate as a Union victory and largely ended Confederate hopes for a negotiated peace.

Robert E. Lee's foray into Pennsylvania to put the war into the North and away from Virginia hastened the end of that war and helped lead us where the U.S. is today.

Lee, a West Point graduate, was a veteran of the Mexican American war some thirty years earlier and a student of the tactics of Napoleon. At the time, all the cadets learned French so they could study Napoleon's words in his native language.

He was considered the greatest general of the time and trained officers of both the Union and Confederate forces traced their training back to him.

Lee was the one who ordered Pickett's charge of 15,000 men across an open field. Aligned shoulder to shoulder, their line stretched for more than a mile. In prior times, it could have been a magnificent scene, breaking through the Union center and decimating the boys in blue.

Instead, Pickett's troops were cut to ribbons with only 150 troops ever actually getting to the Union line. Why was this charge doomed from the beginning? How did the heretofore brilliant general make this enormous mistake?

Because he did not change.

These sorts of tactics had worked well for both the Mexican War and in the early years of the Civil War. Every General of the Army of the Potomac was defeated early on. (Lincoln replaced five of them until he finally found a surly, persistent, innovative leader in U. S. Grant.) Lee's troops had utter faith in him.

His prior success was his undoing at Gettysburg. The first two days had shaped up to be Confederate "wins," but the fateful third day turned the tide irrevocably to the Union.

What changed? The technology of the musket barrel.

What was before a smooth bore musket that had limited accuracy, and range only up to 100 yards was replaced by a rifled bore that not only increased range up to 1,000 yards, but also increased accuracy. The Union troops had these muskets; the Confederates did not. They were doomed from the beginning.

At the time of Napoleon, the troops would march shoulder to shoulder and not fire until they were close to the enemy line. While the defenders were reloading, the attacking line that had withstood the withering first round would charge before they could get their second shot loaded. This was war at close quarters with swords and hand to hand combat.

Napoleon, himself a student of military history, carried a field library of over 1,000 books with him on military campaigns! He out-studied and outsmarted his foes.

Robert E. Lee had trained in this style of battle and had been successful with it before. He was desperate for a crushing victory and risked virtually everything. His risk-taking and better strategy had been successful before against the Union Army, that was numerically superior and better equipped, even before the rifled muskets. He had outwitted numerous Union generals. He had taken risks because he had no other choice for winning.

The grand charge was part of the Napoleonic tactics he had studied. But the Europeans did not have these rifled muskets some fifty years earlier. Had they, their wars would have been quite different.

Lee, despite his history of brilliant general-ing, lost because he did not change his strategy and tactics to match the technology of the day.

(Source: Take Command: Leadership Lessons of the Civil War by Tom Wheeler)

(As an aside, I suspect the military texts also failed Lee because they pointed out Napoleon's tactics. They left out a key stratagem of Napoleon: take advantage of what your enemy gives you. Napoleon never tried to force a battle in one particular way unless it favored him. That principle was ignored at Gettysburg.)

Businesses today face the same siren song of success—keep doing what has been successful in the past. History shows this strategy ultimately fails because the context and circumstances and society and technology all change. Eventually, what once worked will meet obsolescence. History repeats itself.

Just ask the train industry that once thought its business was trains, not transportation. Ask IBM that once thought its business was mainframe computers, causing them to lose 44 billion in the 1990's and throw hundreds of thousands out of work and almost sink the company until reformed as a computer services company.

Ask Motorola that lost its dominant position in cell phones by waiting too long to switch from analog to digital. Nokia beat them to it and was a market leader for years until they lost their edge and ceded the position to Apple and Samsung.

A simple rule of thumb—either you are innovating and creating your future proactively or you are in the process of dying, succumbing to the change that will eventually overtake you. The speed of change is increasing, making the challenge to keep up with it more daunting. Societies change, technology changes.

How do you keep up?

First, accept the fact that you must embrace change as a lever to an improved, more profitable, more successful practice.

Innovation constipation can kill you.

Second, do not dive headlong into every new whiz-bang. Study it. Does it give you an advantage? Does it leverage your time, money or expertise?

Does it make economic sense now or could you make it so? Will the new way, method, or technology give you other advantages in marketing, client experience, or reduced stress? How long is the learning curve? Does it fit your business values and philosophy?

Third, listen to the marketplace. Read, watch, and listen to society. What do the people you serve want? How can the proposed new method or technology help them and you?

Fourth, don't change just for change's sake. Do change with the times.

Fifth, whatever change you do decide to make, engage with it fully. Learn its uses and applications. Train yourself and your team so they not only understand, but also help those you serve want its benefits.

Sixth, accept the fact that some changes will not be successes. Both Lee and Grant often lost several day battles within a campaign and went on to win that entire campaign.

Seventh, continue searching to innovate, to change, and to enhance. Remember that even good ideas often have as much wrong with them as right with them—at first.

The relentless enjoy victories that others could have had, but did not because they stopped, quit, or basked in the success too long. How relentless are you?

Will you learn the lessons of history?

How Sinking U-Boats Could Lead to Raising Your Boat

The North Atlantic, in the early years of WWII, swallowed many ships sunk at the hands of the German submarines, Unterseeboote, called U-boats.

Stealth and firepower of these war machines almost sank the entire war for the Allies until a new science came into play.

Winston Churchill propelled the British Forces and its Navy to borrow the brilliance and insights that would eventually become one of the keys to defeating the German war machine. Over the raised ire of the conservative military commanders, new methods and models were developed that changed the course of the war.

Physicists, biologists, and mathematicians recruited from British universities acted as British government science advisers that applied their knowledge into new ways to counteract and overpower the Axis powers.

The U-boats were wickedly successful in the early years of the war. Devastation of Britain by choking off its supply lines almost succeeded until new science, statistics, and procedures derived from these brilliant minds reversed the course.

U-boats spent most of their time on the surface when at sea. This improved speed and saved fuel. When British air patrols were sent out, the subs would dive, thus eluding detection beneath the waves.

The planes were painted black on the bottom for night time bombing raids. Simply by painting the undersides white to reflect the water below, the planes took 20-30 percent longer to detect, thus giving the Germans less time to dive out of harm's way. That time differential discovery came about by someone outside of the regular military ranks asking questions—the scientists recruited to aid the war effort.

Another scientist derived statistically that any sub that went below the waves for 15 seconds or longer was unlikely to be sunk by depth charges. Before, depth charges were set to explode at 100 to 200 feet.

They only rarely destroyed the U-boat. The key was to catch them as quickly as possible after diving, before they had time to go deep and in any direction. Depth charges instead were set to go off at just 25 feet down. Sub kills went up 10 times! Science trumped the old ways, bringing smiles to the heretofore-resistant Admiralty.

These experts also were responsible for breaking the code of the Enigma, the German method of encrypting communications among military forces. This was a key to the victories including the invasion of Normandy that later ended the war.

Another scientific breakthrough occurred when a group of British scientists noticed how aircraft disrupted radio signals. It took many years, starting in 1935, for this to become what we know today as radar. This was applied with great effect to the air war, but sadly resisted again by the big wigs in the British Navy until late in the war.

These are but examples of the power of disruptive technology to change the world.

Another such field has arrived. This is called Data Science, the technology of making sense of the morass of data that we can figuratively drown in. It has brought exciting leaps in effectiveness of business methods, marketing, operations, and more.

While it is expensive and new, much of the Fortune 500 are now using these technologies of Big Data, to uncover the most effective marketing and most effective marketing combinations with bigger return on marketing invested. That edge can be a game-changer, allowing dollars to get bigger results per dollar spent.

What can you do to create your own breakthrough using data? Unlike the largest companies around the world that learned long ago to measure the results of their efforts in virtually every dimension, almost all professionals and small businesses skip this or do it severe injustice by keeping only the barest of data points.

Principle for you: measure what you want to improve. Name what matters and figure out how to measure the efforts that bring those results.

The big companies study these data points for information contained therein. They look at trends and the effects of old and new initiatives. They compare and contrast. They look for the previously hidden revelations brought to plain sight by data.

Principle for you: study your data. Look for trends. Respond to the information provided to direct your course, change it, or adapt it to the current situation. What does your data reveal? How can you respond? How should you respond?

The most successful companies are always actively looking to get ahead. The newest trend is the use of big data to figure out how each different marketing method figures into getting results. This tracks how the display ad, email campaign, social media, article published as a result of PR efforts, billboards, weather, con-sumer sentiment, interest rates, and more interact additively to see which ones yield the biggest effects in the buying process—a form of multidimensional marketing chess with billions at stake.

While big data cannot be presently applied to your business or professional practice like "the Bigs" are doing today, you can do FAR more than you have been doing.

Going with your gut is OK AFTER you have looked at reams of salient data. Most small entrepreneurs go with their gut BEFORE having and reviewing those reams of important data.

Why do they do this?

Because they don't have these numbers available to them. Why? Because they have not deemed these important enough. They are. Ask me why I know!

The time, effort, and energy spent gathering and interpreting your numbers are some of the most profit-generating activities you can do. For some, this alone can be the difference between boom-ing and suffering. Your choice.

You can track your important numbers. You can use them to improve your decisions. Why not start doing this better today?

Apple, Differentiation, and Best Practices

What can cell phones teach you? What principles demand to be learned?

Nokia, the Finnish cell phone maker, once was the world's dominant cell phone player. Research in Motion found its niche in business phone territory with the Blackberry by using abandoned pager airwaves to create near real time email communication.

Motorola helped start it all by bringing the first commercial analog cell phones to market before both of these companies existed. Nokia swept to the world's leader by going digital. Now all three are in trouble.

Why? All three were innovative at first. Then, somewhere along the way they forgot what "Brung 'em." They fell into the trap of resting on their success for too long. They were passed by more innovation by a computer company who was a Johnny Come Lately to the game of cell phones. Bam! Apple arrived, but not with just another cell phone. It was so much more—a web browser, camera, voice recorder with apps that allow one to use that "smart" phone to make one's life better—easier, more convenient.

Apple didn't just bring a new cell phone that was incrementally better than other cell phones. Apple brought a whole new category. Essentially they replaced the cell phone with a new phone in a category of its own.

The real brilliance was the innovation of tying the iPhone to apps to iTunes and integrating with the Mac, and now, iCloud. Everything just works. Simplicity. It was that genius of tying all the components together that didn't just jolt cell phone sales forward; it catapulted the whole company forward.

Then came the iPad. More symbiosis of product, design, and ease of use. Now Apple has reached more than 285 BILLION dollars in the bank in reserves.

Let's take a backward look for a moment. The early players in cell phones brought their innovations and then stopped innovating. Instead, they made incremental improvements to the existing technology.

How many cell phone models have you seen touted that were merely a tweak here or there without real substantive difference?! You know the answer: plenty. The lure is to take an innovation and milk it for profits.

That is all well and good except the average company gets caught in the trap of their own success. They begin to implement best practices found among all the other players in their marketplace. They engage consulting companies costing millions of dollars to become more efficient and more profitable.

That is the problem—incremental growth, efforts that eke out a few percentage points of improved profitability.

The real advantage is not being caught in the trap of best practices applied to an innovation and putting real innovation aside.

I am not saying that employing best practices is wrong. The problem with best practices is that, as an industry, everyone implements these same practices that everyone else uses taught by the same consultants that often copy each other!

The result is sameness and loss of meaningful differentiation. There is another word for it —commoditization. Have you noticed what it costs for a new run-of-the-mill cell phone?

A new cell phone costs less than 100 dollars, Apple for nearly 800 dollars. Can you imagine what it does to the bottom line? (There is far more to the story of Apple and I'll save that for another day.)

The key is to change your thinking about best practices and innovation. This is not an either/or decision. One must employ best practices to optimize efficiency and profitability. Just don't get stuck in the incremental gains available there.

It is really a both/and decision and more. It is the combination that ensures not only leading the field in innovation, but also launching your bottom line to new heights. History is littered with businesses, countries, and continents whose people failed to apply the art of playing both sides at once.

Playing both sides at once gives you an advantage that few others dare to employ. But not doing so is tantamount to succumbing to an inevitable demise sometime in the future.

(Sidebar: this is why I work with clients as I do—to innovate and employ best practices at the same time.)

Innovation is the driver of the future. You can either join the movement–smart decision—or stay on the sidelines hoping, stuck in the land of incremental gains—good luck with that.

The Cuban Missile Crisis, Inferential Reasoning, and Discovering Your Edge

I can still remember as a nine-year-old kid, the newspapers blaring headlines about missiles in Cuba. It was a very tense few days. In my little town of Bristol, Tennessee, the local officials decided to practice the city-wide emergency response system with its blaring horns—at 6 AM one morning while this crisis was going on.

I met my father on the stairs as we ducked into the basement of our little house built into the side of a hill.

The horns kept screaming for almost an hour. With each passing minute, I wondered how much longer before the bombs hit. My older brother just slept through the whole thing. My mom stayed in her bed. (She was pretty smart about that in hindsight. The basement would not have made any difference.)

Finally the horns stopped. No sound. The local radio or television did not mention a word about it. Surreal. As you know, negotiations were more than tense. We were at the brink of war. It was averted when the Russians pulled their missiles out.

The world breathed a very big sigh of relief.

Do you know how the U.S. found out the missiles were there? My friend and a member of one of my masterminds, Bill Hammond, told this story. It was from none of the usual sources. No clues were offered there. The missiles had been sneaked into Cuba on ships that seemed to be delivering freight from Russia. Castro had successfully thrown out Batista just three years earlier or so. Russia quickly seized the time to become BFFs (Best Friends Forever, for the uninitiated) with Castro.

The CIA of the U.S. monitored the daily living activities, news, broadcasts, and newspapers in Cuba. For years, one particular soccer team went winless. Nada victories. Then suddenly that same team was winning every game. The record went from 0-10 to 10-0! Something was dramatically different! No team turns around that dramatically. Hmmm.

This is when the CIA applied inferential reasoning. The quick, unexpected change in a sports team fortunes could mean that the team had Russians playing for them. Why would Russians be living in Cuba? To install and run missile batteries? More intelligence came to bear on the situation. The missiles were discovered and a very tense world waited, hopeful that the situation would play out for the best.

It did. The Russians took their missiles out. One report is that the U.S. quietly agreed to take their aging missiles out of Turkey in return.

Fast forward to the hunt for Osama bin Laden.

Since 1993, various teams of CIA operatives searched the Middle East for the kingpin of terrorists. How he was found was by the same inferential reasoning.

The courier for bin Laden was located by tracking down the name most mentioned by the terrorists taken prisoner: Ahmed al Kuwaiti. Finding the courier was accomplished by monitoring the courier's mother's phone! The courier was finally located in Abbottabad, Pakistan, in a house less than a mile from the Pakistan Military Academy that was their version of West Point.

Sixteen-foot-high walls surrounded the house and, strangely, none of the normal phone communications one would expect came out from the house. This alone was one confirmation of suspicious activities by the omissions.

Inferential reasoning is a tool for finding out what others don't know. And it is also a tool you could use to monitor society's response to marketing and communication, to see what a competitor is up to, and even start a new business providing offerings that no one else has, and the culture says is ripe.

By the way, here are two easy questions to remember to hone your inferential reasoning IQ. When evaluating a situation, ask:

* What is happening that shouldn't? The case of the Cuban soccer team.
* What isn't happening that should? The case of Osama bin Laden and the communication silent house. (There were more omissions, by the way, implicating the location of bin Laden.)

Moreover, when you use inferential reasoning as part of your strategic advantage tools, you get information that most ignore that you can put to use to give you an edge.

What should you notice these days? What have you been missing? How can you put it to use?

Silk Armor, Outthinking Your Competition, and Disruptive Innovation

Europe's finest were prepared. They knew the army from Asia was on its way and Europeans had an army to defeat them—the best army they ever assembled. Yet, that army was thoroughly defeated by the Hunnic tribes that swept across the steppes of Russia and the Asian plains through modern day Hungary.

If the two armies stood side by side, and you were laying odds on the winner, you would have certainly picked the traditional, armor-laced troops of Western Europe. They had archers, foot soldiers, and cavalry. This was the composition of all successful armies in Europe at the time. They believed themselves invincible.

Much like the artillery of more modern day warfare, the archers would go in first to soften up the enemy and reduce its numbers. Then the foot soldiers attacked, while the cavalry would be held back until the foot soldiers tired. Then, men on horses would sweep in from the flanks to crush the line and win the battle. This was the standard way to fight.

Everyone in Europe fought this way. The best generals cleverly manipulated their archers, foot soldiers, and cavalry to outwit and sometimes simply overpower their opponents.

The Huns just did not agree. They had their own approach—radical in concept compared to European standards. They did not wear armor, so their horses moved far faster and lasted longer in battle. Additionally, they would use multiple horses in a single day to advance quickly or gain advantage of fresh mounts in battle.

They did not have foot soldiers—everyone was on a horse. They did not have archers per se. All the soldiers were atop a horse. All were archers. They did not fight in lines drawn up to fight against an opposing line. The Huns fought like they hunted; they encircled the enemy.

While they did not have armor made of metal, they did have the protection of silk. Yes, silk. They wore silk and placed it on their horses as well. This did not serve in the same way as metal armor.

Instead, it prevented arrows from creating a gashing wound. The arrows would penetrate, but could be pulled out with far, far less damage.

Since they fought atop horses and fired their arrows at full gallop, they were "too fast" for the stationary archers of Europe who were unaccustomed to hitting moving targets that did not fight in lines.

Some say they were the inventors of the stirrup. These allowed the Hunnic warrior to stand while on horseback and shoot in virtually all directions while moving.

The bows of the Hunnic archers were smaller than the bows used by the Europeans. To further advantage, their bows were recurved composite bows that increased accuracy, speed, force of the arrows, and distance while being lighter. Perfect for someone on a horse.

The Huns were victorious until the Europeans adapted. But this was not easy. Nor was it fast. It took a long time. The advantage remained with the Hunnic tribes for quite some time, allowing the Huns to forge into virtually all of Western and Eastern Europe while creating an eastern European empire of their own.

What are the lessons of this foray into history? And how can you apply these in the here and now? What else should this quick recount of historic advantage teach you? (I'll give you that one right now: history is important for the lessons it teaches that you can apply in the present while giving you a modicum of prediction of the future as you come to understand human nature. Human nature remains a constant, even while technology grows exponentially.)

The Huns outthought their adversaries, who mistakenly considered them savages. They used disruptive innova-tions in warfare processes by disregarding the "accepted way" of battle, confusing the opponents, and thus further slowing them down, sometimes to the point of freezing up.

They used speed to surprise and overpower their enemies, utilizing lightning-fast (for the time) forces that could fight in one part of the battlefield and then quickly strike another. Their opponents simply did not move that fast.

The Hunnic battle gear consisting of composite bows, large and small swords, lassoes, and lances, gave them the advantage in close quarters and in distance attacks. They had superior armaments.

The Hun troops were safer from injury and death, aided by their silk armor and speed tactics of war. They trained to be on horseback with composite bow from childhood. It was part of the fabric of their society.

All of these advantages led them to endless victories and a prominent place in the memories of the peoples of today.

Now here are five questions for you:

* How can you create unfair, insurmountable advantages?
* How can you use speed as your ally?
* How could you use training to better "arm your troops" to overpower the opposition?
* What process can you create that gives you competitive edge that others will ignore (at least for now)?
* How could you redefine the battlefield with your competitors to give you victory by virtual default?

Can you use Hunnic history to propel your business or professional practice forward?

By the way, how many people that you know use the fulcrum of the past to leverage their present to create the winning future?

Why not you? You never know, you just might outthink your competition.

In Closing

Important Words to Finish Off For Now

In these pages, you have gotten a distinctly different point of view and some workable tools to help you better your practice.

Unfortunately, most dentists are still stuck with their bits and pieces when thinking about growing and running a practice for profit. A majority of doctors have so many misconceptions about the business of practice it's scary.

It's scary because these mistaken considerations, flawed thinking and beliefs that just aren't true are near certain to shackle your practice from ever growing to its full potential. This is why so many doctors are struggling.

Every time I go to a large dental conference I am struck by how almost everyone in attendance is approaching his or her practice the wrong way. They continue to try a little bit here and a little piece there.

Here's a thought: if this opportunity seeking way worked so well, wouldn't every doctor be a lot better off? Are they? If you really look behind the facade of "I am doing great," another story can be found that few doctors want to admit to themselves – that they are struggling and worried; hopeful that the next bit or piece they get will be the one that fixes it all (the magic silver bullet fix). Hope is not a plan. Wishes work in fairy tales.

Lack of fundamental business building knowledge is the fundamental cause of so much struggling and time wasting. It is sad really. This is the reason why the majority of doctors fail to achieve their dreams even if they buy lots of programs, whiz-bang technol-ogy, the most up-to- date products and work very hard.

Look, hard work is a given. But it is the type of work; the right kind of knowledge and its application that makes the hard work bear fruit.

True practice success can never be found with a "bits and pieces" type approach. "Seeking the next opportunity" over and over just costs you a lot of money, drains your time away and leaves you with that "inner growl" sometimes directed at yourself and other times directed to all those around you.

This is like digging for diamonds in a coal mine.
All you get is grimy. If you do it long enough, you'll get your very own version of practice black lung disease. I know from past experience that my unique perspective and systems can make a tremendous difference in your practice, as it has had for so many of my coaching clients.

I can't sit on the sidelines anymore and allow so many dreams to fall in the ditch due to misunderstanding how successful prac-tices are built.

Not knowing what to do or how do it and why to do it in your practice is the most expensive ignorance there is. And it this lack of workable knowledge and its application that makes you and the entire field prey for the corporations that have already entered out field.

They see profits off the work you do that you are losing right now because of your lack of knowledge and knowhow. Take look at what has happened in other fields.

The local corner drug store has virtually gone away as the big box versions like CVS and Walgreens have taken over backed up big dollars coming from Wall Street.

Optometry can now be had inside Target, Sears, JC Penny as well as large national eye care chains like Pearl Vision, Lens Crafters and even Walgreens.

Corporations and hospitals own over 60% of physician offices.

Cottage industry thinking, which has pervaded healthcare, just doesn't work anymore. The proof stares you in the face. It will be very costly to turn a blind eye.

Sadly, some doctors will. They will say to themselves that "It won't happen to me," like the smoker who kids himself into thinking he won't get cancer and then when he does, he acts surprised. Another one is "I'll retire before it affects me." You had better be retiring in the next ninety days because it definitely affects the value of your practice and your ultimate future.

Doesn't it make sense to act now to get the security of a strategically designed practice and its proven business methods that extract all the profits that should be yours?

Doesn't it make sense to gain that knowing confidence of the Master Dentist who makes time and money work for him instead of being owned by the practice?

Doesn't it make sense to regain your good feeling mojo that has been zapped and drained by bits and pieces thinking?

If you said yes or even maybe to the above questions, I suggest you go immediately to www.MasterYourPractice.com. Here you'll find more resources including an online training that takes the content of this book further.

I wish you all the best,

Dr. Charles Martin, but you can call me Charley

We help Dentists and Orthodontists create a different kind of practice with a steady, consistent, predictable flow of new patients who want to say yes to your best care so you make more money without the frustration and overwhelm.

MasterYourPractice.com

www.ingramcontent.com/pod-product-compliance
Lightning Source LLC
Chambersburg PA
CBHW052312220526
45472CB00001B/84

* 9 7 8 1 9 8 1 2 7 4 2 4 6 *